The History of the Sixteen Karmapas of Tibet

The History of the Sixteen Karmapas of Tibet

KARMA THINLEY
The Fourth Karma Thinleypa

Edited with an essay by David Stott
Illustrated by Namkha Tashi
Foreword by Chögyam Trungpa
Introduction by Reginald A. Ray

1980 Prajñā Press BOULDER

Shambhala Publications, Inc.
2129 13th Street
Boulder, Colorado 80302
www.shambhala.com

Printed in the United States of America

Shambhala Publications makes every effort to print on acid-free, recycled paper.

Shambhala Publications is distributed worldwide by Penguin Random House, Inc., and its subsidiaries.

LIBRARY OF CONGRESS CATALOGING-IN-PUBLICATION DATA

Karma Thinley, Lama Wangchhim.
The history of the sixteen Karmapas of Tibet.
1. Kar-ma-pa lamas—Tibet—Biography. 2. Kar-ma-pa (Sect)—History.
I. Stott, David. II. Title.
BQ7682.9.A2K285 80-179
294.3'61'0922
ISBN 978-1-57062-644-9
BVG 01

CONTENTS

FOREWORD

THE PRACTICING LINEAGE of the Kagyu tradition remains the crown jewel of the contemplative Buddhist world. The examples and life styles of great teachers of this tradition have inspired countless practitioners, such that their lives could be further devoted to meditative disciplines. The Karmapas are particularly the great pillars of the Kagyu tradition, who have enabled the practicing lineage to continue in spite of political, social and economic obstacles.

Karma Thinley, Rinpoche, is a very close friend and student of mine. I appreciate his insight and wisdom in revealing to us the true stories of the lineage of the Karmapas. No doubt this book will benefit its readers; they should read it with inspiration and devotion.

I remain a servant and propagator of the Kagyu tradition,

Chögyam Trungpa

Vajracarya the Venerable
Chögyam Trungpa, Rinpoche
Boulder, Colorado
21 February 1980

PREFACE

"The teachings of the Karmapas will last as long as the teachings of a thousand Buddhas."

—Karma Pakshi

THE GREAT *TERTON,* Chogyur Lingpa, predicted that the sixteenth or seventeenth Karmapa would one day cross the ocean. True to his prediction the teachings of the sixteenth Karmapa have spread to reach the Western continent. In fact, Gyalwa Karmapa has now traveled twice around the world and given teachings and initiations to many followers and established numerous Kagyu centers.

In Tibet there were nine Buddhist sects that followed the teachings of the *hīnayāna, mahāyāna* and *vajrayāna:* Gelugpa, founded by the Mañjuśrī emanation, Tsongkhapa; Nyingmapa, founded by Vajrācārya Padmasambhava, King Trisong Detsun and Abbot Śāntarakṣita; Kadampa, founded by Atīśa and Gyalwa Dromtonpa; Sakyapa, founded by Drogmi Lotsawa and Konchog Gyalpo; Kagyupa, founded by Nāropa and Marpa Lotsawa; Chod ("Cutting Through Ego"), founded by the lady *siddhā,* Machig Labkyi Dronma; Shijay ("Pacifying Suffering"), founded by Dampa Sangye; Shangpa Kagyu, founded by Khyungpo Naljor; and the Urgyen Nyendrup, founded by the *mahāsiddha* and *paṇḍita,* Urgyenpa Rinchen Pal.

At present surviving in strength are the Gelugpa, Sakyapa, Kagyupa and Nyingmapa. All follow the same basic teachings of Buddhism brought from India to Tibet at the price of great material and human resources over the centuries.

Basically all of these sects are holders of *vajrayāna* transmissions from Vajradhara and passed down to the guru. The *lama* is in fact a manifestation of Vajradhara and, therefore, of very great importance. That is why in the past Tibetan Buddhism has been referred to by some as "lamaism." The term refers to this aspect of Tibetan Buddhism.

If you study one sect then you will understand all sects. There are no important differences in their teachings. A Tibetan proverb says that when you cast a flower into the *maṇḍala,* the deity it lands on is yours. Similarly whichever lineage you first meet and take teachings from becomes most important to you. You must learn its teachings correctly and receive the transmission of the lineage. It is also important to know the history of the lineage.

There are many books on the lives of the Karmapas written in Tibetan. Quite often people have asked me to retell the life stories of the Karmapas. I am not able to do something new that would be better than existing histories but some of these were written centuries ago and are not complete. Out of several books I collected stories from each life and translated them into English with the help of Stanley Fefferman and John McCann. The manuscript was then edited by Jampa Thaye (David Stott), who is engaged in Ph.D. research at the University of Manchester. Namkha Tashi (Christopher Banigan) did the illustrations, after the most famous paintings of the Kagyu lineage, the work of Karshu Gonpo Dorje, brought by Sangye Nyenpa Rinpoche from Kham as a gift to the sixteenth Karmapa.

In the West there are many Kagyu *lamas* and students. As a gift to those interested in the Karma Kagyu lineage and devoted to Gyalwa Karmapa we have collected and translated stories of the first sixteen Karmapa incarnations. I hope this book helps to introduce an understanding of the study and training of the *bodhisattva* and of how the lineage has been transmitted from the beginning up to now. Each Karmapa has had a slightly different effect as a *bodhisattva* in order to help sentient beings. Whatever merit gained from having done this is dedicated to our world family—that it might have peace, happiness, freedom from sickness, war and starvation and the complete achievement of enlightenment and the *bodhisattva* state.

Introduction

THE BIOGRAPHIES contained in this volume may strike the reader as strange, to say the least. They come from the alien and seemingly impenetrable world of medieval Tibet. They are cast in the psychological and literary idiom of a country and culture which, more than any other, have symbolized for the Western world everything that is incomprehensible, bizarre and fantastic. In modern times, Tibet has come to represent the mirror opposite of the experience we as Westerners have of our world. In approaching these stories then, one may well ask, why bother? What possible value can such tales have for us Westerners?

The answer would seem to depend a great deal on the reader. Certainly, on the most superficial level, we can read these stories as fanciful tales. As we have with the religious literature of other non-Western peoples, we can read these biographies for the play of imagination they allow. We can look to them for intimations of another world and for the entry they provide into realms of magic and mystery that ordinarily elude us in our day to day lives. As psychologists and students of culture have suggested, this is no insignificant function. Far from being pure entertainment, stories of this kind can provide needed relief from the claustrophobia of the completely familiar and unextraordinary world we too often experience.

If we want to go further, we may find something more in these stories. As cultural anthropologists in this century have shown, stories such as these from non-Western spiritual traditions are more than expressions of fantasy. They embody forms of experience and expression of the culture from which they come. In this volume we are confronted—in some very real sense—with what the world of the traditional Tibetan was like. We may find the atmosphere, events and people depicted in these biographies rather singular and unlikely, but in fact they represent the natural state of affairs in medieval Tibet. These stories provide a window into this medieval world with its peculiarly Tibetan idioms, values and interests. Of course, to gain some intuition into this world and to begin to appreciate it, we need to put aside for a moment our Western canons of what is real and what is not. But in this day and age, such a suspension of judgment is not as hard as it used to be. And, the reward of seeing how differently the world can be experienced in other cultural contexts would seem to be well worth the effort.

Cultural anthropology stops at this point of appreciation, but one can go further, and this leaves us with the most difficult of issues. The oft quoted line from Rudyard Kipling, "East is East and West is West and never the twain shall meet,"[1] is more than an aphorism. It is a fundamental assumption and presupposition that is deeply rooted in Western consciousness. Anyone who works in the field of non-Western religion as anthropologist or orientalist is acutely aware of the general paranoia existing in our culture of non-Western peoples and traditions. In looking at non-Western traditions this is best exemplified by the scholarly attempt to maintain objectivity by "not getting too close" or compromising one's identity as a Westerner. Even C. G. Jung, for all of his appreciation of non-Western spirituality, frequently expressed his fear that too intimate a contact with non-Western traditions would lead to an unhealthy rejection of our identity as Westerners. The excesses and inaccuracies of pseudo-Asian cultists in this culture would seem to justify this Western paranoia of Asian spirituality.

However, these two approaches—that of the sceptical scholar who rejects such intimacy out of hand or that of the cultist who thinks he can become a Hindu or a Tibetan—both fail to explore the really interesting and significant question. Does the kind of spiritual world described in, for example, the Tibetan religion of these biographies exist solely and exclusively within the Tibetan frame of reference? Or does it have some implication beyond that, which tests the boundaries of our Western experience? In other words, do the psychological and spiritual limits of our Western reality inhere necessarily in the very make-up of ourselves and our culture or are they to some extent self imposed? This is the most basic and fundamental of questions, and how we answer it will determine the way in which we read these stories, and what we find in them.

The Visions of the Karmapas

The biographies that follow are not easy to read, and a few guidelines are necessary to orient the reader to their style and contents. To begin with, these are not biographies in our modern Western sense of the word. All biographies are selective, based on a particular view of what is significant. Unlike most modern Western biographies which depict primarily secular events, the biographies of the Karmapas concern a certain fundamental dimension of Tibetan life, namely the connection between man and the divine—their relationship, their tensions and their communication. To say this is not to say much, unless we realize that these stories actually recount the way in which the life was experienced in traditional Tibet, particularly by figures such as the Karmapas. For these individuals, the main thread running through their lives, was their interaction with the spiritual world. And the central moments in this interaction were their visions. One could well say that to tell the story of the significant events in the life of a Karmapa is to recount those visions, with the understanding they embody and the activity they produce. In fact, it is those visions that form the main subject matter of these biographies.

This being so, something should be said about these spiritual experiences and the way in which they provide the foundation of the Karmapa biographies. According to the *vajrayāna* tradition—the form of Buddhism which the Karmapas represent—the subject has two aspects to it: first, the preparation that must take place in order for an individual to be receptive to such experiences; second, the progressive training in Buddhist meditation through which one's insight and intuition are actually developed. This progressive training occurs in three stages, conventionally labeled in Buddhist terminology *hīnayāna* (the lesser vehicle), *mahāyāna* (the greater vehicle) and *vajrayāna* (the diamond vehicle). In order to properly understand the visions of the Karmapas we need to look briefly at this preparation and "three-*yāna*" meditation training.

The first point that needs to be made is that the "visions" that play so central a role in these biographies are in a way quite ordinary and down to earth. Unlike the experience of the Western mystic who is swept into unearthly realms, the spiritual insights of the Karmapas concern the mundane realities of human life. In fact, they represent the overtones of ordinary experience that are usually hidden from the eye. This point is important, because it is consistent with the general Buddhist view that there is no other reality than that which presents itself immediately to experience. Even descriptions of deities or discussions of buddha-realms are nothing other than ways of talking about the subleties of actual, literal experience as it is always at hand.

At the same time, much of the teaching of the Karmapas' *vajrayāna* Buddhist tradition is described as "self-secret." This refers to the fact that while people outside of the tradition may read its texts, generally their literal import remains well-hidden. One might think that this self-secrecy exists because of a technical reason such as, for example, a lack of familiarity with traditional idioms or vocabulary. But, actually, the reason lies in quite another direction. The Karmapas' tradition exists to provide access to a direct insight into reality, into "things as they are" *(yathābhūtam),* as it is technically phrased. And, as we have noted, this "reality" is not the abstract reality of another sphere, but rather the concrete reality that continually presents itself as experience. Why, one may ask, should something seemingly so natural and so ordinary be secret? The answer is simple. Reality, according to Buddhism, is not grasped by thought. It is rather seen only by a mind that is clear, open and without preoccupation. But where is such a mind found? In fact, it is the habitual tendency of the human mind to be taken up with plans, views and projects. Driven on by the hope of gaining and the fear of losing, the mind is never still, but always on the move. This ceaseless activity never gives intuition room to develop, and intuition is itself the gateway to the world "as it is." The *raison d'etre* of the Karmapas' tradition is to provide people with a path to transcending the self-absorption of preconceptions and preoccupations, so that intuition may unfold and the world as it is may show itself without stain. Until that path is entered, the world "as it is" remains secret.

The first step in the development of insight—and a theme that runs throughout the Karmapa biographies—is renunciation. Renunciation is based on the awareness that human beings constantly avoid seeing things as they are, preferring instead to strike for comfort, security and confirmation. Growing recognition of the incessant self-seeking machinations of ego leads to increasing disgust with the whole process, and a longing to let it go. Renunciation is the initial inspiration for working on oneself to eliminate self-deception. In the Buddhist tradition, it is said that simply recognizing the problem is not enough to achieve the goal. One must work on oneself through practices that train the mind. For Buddhism, this work is carried out through the practice of meditation. It is this practice that develops the increasing clarity of vision that is described in the training of the three *yānas.* And it is this practice that forms the heart of the Karmapas' own journey and of what they have to teach others.

The first level of vision or insight is called *vipaśyanā* or "clear seeing," developed through the meditative practices of the *hīnayāna.* The practice of *hīnayāna* is to sit cross-legged, and to rest one's attention lightly on one's breath, with awareness of one's environment. Through this simple practice, one's thought processes—which in the beginning are incessant and without breaks—begin to slow down. After a great deal of practice, gaps in one's thought processes begin to occur. These gaps bring a clarity of insight, *vipaśyanā,* that is not contaminated by preconceptions or expectations.

What is it that appears in the *vipaśyanā* experience? Simply the ordinary world, in its infinite detail, its multitudinous complexity and its unending interrelation. Sounds, sights, sensations, thoughts, the nature of situations, one's own and others' motivations, all show themselves, free from one's hopes and fears. The world in its many facets begins to stand out starkly in one's experience. In Buddhist tradition, it is said that this experience cuts through ego because it reveals the world as it actually is, not as one thinks or wants it to be. In light of this experience, one's own personal version of things is shown up for what it is: not reality, but one's own erroneous, insubstantial, and unconvincing thought. It is also said to be the first taste of enlightenment, because what is seen has nothing to do with ego. When the following biographies mention the *hīnayāna* training of Dusum Khyenpa, Rangjung Dorje and the other Karmapas, they are referring to this first stage in the development of the Karmapas' "vision."

When *hīnayāna* training is firmly rooted and *vipaśyanā* has begun to challenge ordinary, egoistic patterns, the next level of training begins, that of the *mahāyāna* or "great vehicle." Whereas in *vipaśyanā* the world is seen in its detail and complexity, in the *mahāyāna* vision of *śūnyatā* (emptiness), the groundlessness of experience begins to stand out. For all of its sharpness and clarity, *hīnayāna vipaśyanā* has its limitations. The practices leading to it are carried out for one's own sake, one's individual salvation. It also conveys implicitly the impression that something definite has been achieved, and it provides a resting place—albeit refined and subtle—for one to cling to. In short, *hīnayāna* carries with it a subtle version of ego. It replaces gross egotism with a more spiritual version of ego's territory. And it has its own kind of hope and fear—hope of further *vipaśyanā* experience and fear of falling back into the ignorance of *saṃsāric* neurosis. The next level of training, that of the *mahāyāna,* seeks to work through the subtle spiritual clinging of the *hīnayāna.* How can such an aim be accomplished? The answer is through further renunciation. Here, the goal of freeing oneself from *saṃsāra,* of attaining certain experiences, and of finding a reference point in *vipaśyanā* must all be abandoned. And, again, such an aim cannot be accomplished simply through recognition of the problem, but must be achieved bit by bit through meditation practice.

The *mahāyāna* practice is called *lojong* (Tib.: *blo.sbyong*), "mind training," and it has two aspects, one absolute and the other relative. The absolute practice involves continuing with the sitting practice of meditation. Through this practice, one begins to gain more familiarity with the unconditioned, non-ego dimension of the mind, termed absolute *bodhicitta* (enlightened mind). This leads to less fear of agitated and anxious states of mind, and one begins to sense the unconditioned quality present throughout one's experience, whether *saṃsāric* or otherwise. This undercuts the apparent duality between *saṃsāra* and *nirvāṇa,* and gives rise to the experience of groundlessness, without any reference points at all. Inseparable from the absolute practice is the relative practice, called relative *bodhicitta,* in which—through "meditation in action"—the practitioner works with other people. The relative practice is grounded in the trust and insight that is developed in the absolute practice and, moving into the sphere of activity, is aimed at trying to help others. The practice involves continually giving up personal territory and assisting others in whatever way one can. Instead of blaming others, one takes the blame of situations on oneself. Instead of avoiding their problems, one takes on their pain. Instead of seeking good for oneself, one seeks the gain of others, in particular, and most especially, their liberation from *saṃsāra.* Through this demanding practice, one begins to realize that the instinct for self-survival can be transcended in favor of something much broader and more expansive. Having abandoned the reference point even of one's own spiritual survival and advancement by working for the salvation of others, one attains the same groundlessness in action that one attained in sitting practice, with no reference points whatever. When the following biographies speak of the *mahāyāna* training of the Karmapas, they are referring to this training.

In the Buddhist tradition of the Karmapas, the *hīnayāna* and *mahāyāna* training provide foundation and preparation for the *vajrayāna* or *tantric* vehicle itself. From the viewpoint of this highest Buddhist teaching, just as the *hīnayāna* had its limitations and required further renunciation, so the same thing can be said of the *mahāyāna.* The strength of the *mahāyāna* is its discovery of groundlessness and absolute nonreference point. But, according to the *vajrayāna,* this discovery in itself becomes a preoccupation. In a tremendously subtle way, a process of discrimination, selection and distortion is still taking place. Experience is evaluated according to whether or not it is without ground. If it is not, then according to the *mahāyāna,* it is lacking in spirituality, and must be corrected by the viewpoint of *śūnyatā.* Here, according to the *vajrayāna,* is the same dualism that was found in the *hīnayāna,* albeit on a much more subtle level: this *vajrayāna* criticism is framed in an analogy by the great *tantric* poet Saraha:

He who does not enjoy the senses purified
And practices only the Void,
Is like a bird that flies up from a ship
And then wheels round and lands back there again.[2]

Further renunciation must take place as one enters the *vajrayāna*. One must see the sticking point of the *mahāyāna* adherence to *śūnyatā* and be willing to abandon attachment to the duality of spiritual and unspiritual. Even the reference point of no reference point must be given up. If this is done, what is left? Simply experience as it is in itself, with no preconceptions, no expectations, no evaluations. Experience simply shows itself for what it is, with its particular shape and contours, textures and overtones. As the *vajrayāna* tradition says, the world of experience rightly seen possesses the qualities of nowness, emptiness, luminosity and resplendency. The nowness comes from *hīnayāna* training, still in full force. Having seen the distinction between experience and thoughts, one knows how to bring oneself back to the present, and no longer lives in past memory or future expectation. The emptiness comes from *mahāyāna* training, where one has learned how to overcome longing for solid ground. The luminosity and resplendency refers specifically to the *vajrayāna*. The world is luminous because, when one no longer has thoughts about things, they appear with great vividness. The world is resplendent because it is sacred, and is filled with awesomeness and power.

As in the previous *yānas*, the full realization of the *vajrayāna* is not accomplished without thorough and arduous training. As in the *mahāyāna*, *vajrayāna* practice has both an absolute or "formless" and a relative or "form" aspect. The formless practice involves continued "formless" meditation of just sitting, and exploring emptiness more completely. The form aspect has two related types of practice, one a kind of sitting meditation, the other meditation in action. Both of these have to do with the *vajrayāna devatās* or deities, and this topic requires explanation. In the *vajrayāna*, one's own unconditioned intelligence—discovered in the *mahāyāna*—is given a visual and iconographic form. This is done to enable one to relate directly with this intelligence, beyond the trammels of ego. This is known as visualizing oneself as the *devatā*. Secondly, the external world is figured also in the form of a *devatā*, to underline and embody its sacredness. The *devatā* that is oneself and the *devatā* as the external world are, moreover, the same deity, and this brings up a point we shall explore further below: that one's innermost world and that of external phenomena are not two, but rather two expressions of one reality. In the form practice of the *vajrayāna,* both sitting meditation and meditation in action, oneself and the external world are seen as the *devatā.* Formless and form practice are bound together in the understanding that the *devatā* has two aspects: one of form, the other formless. The path of the *vajrayāna* involves developing more and more complete trust in experience—form and formless—as the reality of the *devatā*—in other words as complete, perfect and without stain.

The biographies that follow are, as noted above, filled with accounts of "visions" of deities. The foregoing should suggest what kind of visions these are. They are embodiments of the individual's own deepest, unconditioned intelligence and of the sacredness of the world itself. To see the *devatās* is to encounter these elemental aspects of existence. When self-doubt arises, the *devatās* provide some more profound understanding. When confusion about the world holds sway, the *devatās* speak for the simplicity and dignity of things as they are. The reason that each Karmapa has so much to do with the *vajrayāna* deities is that he speaks for the basic and unimpeachable dignity of human beings and for the goodness of the world. In the stories that follow, we see the Karmapas engaged in teaching their students the path to the realization of these facts. And we see them working with situations of social and political chaos and suffering, to restore harmony, mutual respect and happiness. As one reads through these stories with their play back and forth between "visions" and activity, it is essential to keep in mind the intimate relation existing between the two: because the Karmapas see the good of people and of the world, they have a vision to be actualized in social and political realms. Because of their relation to the *devatās,* as expressions of unconditioned, egoless intelligence and the "isness" of the world, they have the personal resources to actualize that vision.

Vision, then, in the sense used in these stories, has quite a different meaning from the common usage in the history of religions. The vision of the Karmapas, based on their *hīnayāna, mahāyāna* and *vajrayāna* training, is actually profound insight into what is, rather than into what could or should be. It is this "isness," of the egoless intelligence of people and the sacredness of the world, that gives the Karmapas' vision so much significance and so much power. Their mission is to bring out in the world what is already there—to teach people their basic goodness and to teach respect for the sacredness of what is. It is this vision, along with the practice to realize it, that make the Karmapas such singular and exceptional people, and make their biographies worthy of study.

Magic

The preceding elucidation of the earthy and realistic nature of the visions of the Karmapas does not quite resolve all of our major difficulties in attempting to understand these biographies. That point having been made, a question immediately presents itself. If the realization and teaching of the Karmapas is really so ordinary and so in tune with "things as they are," then what possible explanation can there be for the prominent role played by magic in these stories? For even cursory reading of these accounts shows them to be filled with all kinds of magical displays. According to the biographies, Dusum Khyenpa miraculously traveled to Ceylon where he received teaching from the Mahāsiddha Vajraghaṇṭā. He was also known for his extraordinary healing powers. Karma Pakshi was able to move a huge statue merely through the power of his meditation. Rangjung Dorje was able to speak on the day of his birth. He also gained mastery of the field of astrology and wrote a classic on the subject after seeing the entire universe contained within his body. As well, he is remembered for having the ability to change deleterious climatic conditions. Rolpe Dorje manifested clear, detailed, and accurate memories of his life in his previous incarnation. He was also able to heal himself of sickness merely by meditating on Bhaiṣajyaguru, the medicine buddha. Dezhin Shegpa exhibited the power of reading others' thoughts. When he visited the Ming emperor, Yung Lo, material objects appeared in space, apparitions of *arhats* were seen walking through the streets, a monk was observed flying through the sky, a rain of flowers fell on the emperor's palace, and the clouds took on the form of *vajrayāna* deities. Thongwa Donden knew the date of his death well before its occurrence. Chodrag Gyatsho through his vision was able to locate certain hidden valleys as a refugee during political conflict. Mikyo Dorje left footprints in the rock floors of various meditation caves at Kampo Gangra, as well as carving a stone statue that was able to speak. Through his magical power, he brought an end to an epidemic of leprosy in southern Tibet. Yeshe Dorje once emanated several forms of himself, each of which gave teachings to the individuals present. Dudul Dorje was able to create at long distance a rain of barley from the sky over a monastery at Powo Gyaldzong in need of blessing.

The accounts of magical events and activities in the Karmapa biographies reaches a culmination in the story of the present Karmapa, Rangjung Rigpe Dorje, born in 1923 and currently residing at Rumtek monastery near Gangtok, Sikkim, India. Before his birth, it is said that he disappeared for a time from his mother's womb. On the day of his birth, all kinds of unusual natural phenomena occurred. While studying with his *guru,* he recounted to him the stories of his previous incarnations. At Drong Tup he left footprints in the water which, it is said, can still be seen, winter or summer. As he performed a Padmasambhava ceremony, the *tormas* on the shrine appeared to burst into flame. He brought an end to a severe drought afflicting a monastery in Nangchen. At Pangphug monastery, he left footprints in stone. His dog and horse also left footprints in the rock. At Benchen monastery, he caused the statue of a horse to neigh. Through his vision, when escaping from Tibet, he enabled his party to escape from closely pursuing Chinese forces.

The preceding examples are only a few of the many that might be cited to illustrate the prominent role played by magic in these biographies. These and the other similar occurrences leave the Western reader with a crucial question. What sense can be made of all of these examples of magic in the Karmapa biographies? Do they represent exceptions of the reality-orientation of the stories? Are they lapses in the integrity of the accounts and must they be excised for the stories to be properly understood? Is the incidence of magic due, for example, to the entry of "popular" elements into the lives? Or is it a literary device, perhaps added later, to enhance the prestige of the central figure? These questions resolve themselves into a single, central issue. Are these occurrences of magic integral to the biographies, or are they not? Are they or are they not essential to an understanding of who the Karmapas are and what they do?

For a long time, Western scholars have judged that occurrences of this kind in the history of religions are marks of a pre-logical, pre-scientific, or otherwise inferior mentality. The ground for such a viewpoint obviously lies deeply rooted in Western Christendom where magic has often traditionally been classified as a "work of darkness." A more secular manifestation of the same approach is the enlightenment view that magic in religion is proof of its infantile or demented character. Nineteenth and early twentieth-century scholars followed in the same track. Frazer saw magic as an early stage of religion that was based on an inadequate understanding of reality. And Malinowski found it accompanied by a lower level of intelligence. Closer to home, contemporary scholars of Tibetan religion have rendered similar judgments on the occurrence of magic in the Indian and Tibetan *vajrayāna.* It seems generally agreed that the incidence of magic in *tantric* biographies of the Karmapa type render them largely unworthy of historical credence. So far, then, the Western reader seems to be left with two choices. On the one hand, he may decide that the incidence of magic in the biographies is not essential. In this case, he may remove the examples of magic and then take the biographies seriously as accounts of the Karmapas. On the other hand, he may decide the incidence of magic is essential to the biographies. If this be so, then the nature of the accounts as real stories of real people is thrown into doubt.

As more is learned about Tibetan Buddhism, it is becoming increasingly clear that neither of these two viewpoints is adequate. On the one hand, magic seems to be quite integral to the Karmapa biographies. On the other, these stories also seem to be historical in the most basic sense of the word. They are chronicles of people's experience of their lives and their world. How can both points be true? The starting point of our understanding must begin with simple fact. The world pictured in these biographies is an accurate representation of how life was experienced in Tibet, up to the Chinese invasion of the 1950s. Magical occurrences of the type described in these biographies were regular if extraordinary experiences of the people of Tibetan culture, from the lowliest, most uneducated peasant, to the most sophisticated, most highly educated *lamas*. And these were not haphazard occurrences. They proceeded in an organic way from the very nature of reality as experienced by the Tibetans. Furthermore, the ability to produce magical phenomena was dependent on an individual's psychological and spiritual development. We know all of this to be the case, not only from traditional literature, but also from contemporaries, both Western and Tibetan. Western observers have chronicled the extent to which magical occurrences of the kind cited above were regular parts of life for the Tibetans and, in some cases, for themselves, in Tibet. And one knows contemporary *lamas* of scrupulous and profound integrity who talk quite simply about such occurrences as a natural part of their lives in Tibet and after. From all of this it would appear that the Karmapa biographies are quite faithful and accurate when they represent magic as a basic part of the Karmapas' lives. This having been said, can we say more?

In the past, Western scholars have randomly lumped together examples such as those cited above under the general category of "magic." We must remember that "magic" is a Western term and a Western concept and, in fact, is used to cover a wide range of heterogeneous phenomena occurring in world religions. What is it, then, that has led scholars to group such phenomena under the single rubric of "magic"? The one common feature of these phenomena seems to be that the Western scientific world view has had no explanation for these occurrences. As it turns out in fact, the phenomena that we have grouped under the term "magic" are very diverse. In order to gain further insight into the role of magic in the Karmapa's lives, it will be useful to briefly elucidate this diversity. As we shall see, a closer look at these phenomena shows that they fall into a few fairly clear and discrete categories. Moreover, these categories are not peculiar to the lives presented in this volume, but are entirely traditional, going all the way back to the biographies of the Indian *mahāsiddhas,* the *vajrayānist* antecedents and prototypes of the Karmapas, and in many cases back to Buddha Śākyamuni himself.

The phenomena that we have been labeling "magic" in the preceding pages fall into two large divisions, each with sub-categories. On the one hand, there are extraordinary phenomena that are mainly psychological in nature. This category includes ability to see deities, prescience, various types of yogic powers, ability to experience others' thoughts, and the *tulku's* (Tib.: *sprul.sku*) remembrance of former lives. The second large category contains phenomena that express an inherent connection between mind and external world. This grouping includes psychosomatic powers, ability to move matter, divination, some phenomena of synchronicity, and the ability to affect climate. It is important to note that these two broad classifications of extraordinary abilities are not Tibetan or even *vajrayāna* in origin, but go back through *mahāyāna* times to the earliest days of Buddhism.

Extraordinary Phenomena Mainly Psychological in Nature

The first large group of extraordinary phenomena are mainly psychological in nature. They are all bound together by the fact that they all have to do with ways of experiencing reality. In that sense, they refer back to the preceding section of this introduction on "visions." This group of phenomena all proceed from an extraordinary openness and subtlety of experience, developed through the process of meditation. By having given up normal mental preoccupations, experience begins to appear with increasing clarity and subtlety. As that stage reaches a high degree of development, some of the phenomena that we have labeled as "magic" begin to come into play.

Reading minds. It is said in the biographies that Dezhin Shegpa had the ability to see others' thoughts. This power is one mentioned throughout the history of Buddhism from earliest times. It is one of the classical *siddhis* or mental abilities that arises from attaining a high level of egolessness. Experience, according to Buddhism, is not purely individual, but environmental in character. When a high degree of openness and receptivity is attained, one can pick up the experience of others.

Prescience. Thongwa Donden's biography tells us that he foresaw his own death. Again, this motif is first found in the biography of Śākyamuni Buddha and reappears over and over throughout the history of Buddhism. In Tibetan Buddhism, it was a longstanding tradition that *lamas* would often predict the time of their death, sometimes months or even years in advance. This ability is one example of the power of prescience that is described throughout Buddhist tradition. From the Buddhist viewpoint, the power of prescience is explained as based on the interconnection of present and future. Events and trends that will arise in the future are already contained in the present as *karmic* seeds. Moreover, the particular way that these seeds will unfold is dependent on the surrounding causal context, as that also develops out of the present. It is said that enlightened people have such an immense breadth of vision that they can see future developments in a flash.

The Ability to See Deities. The Karmapas in general are credited with the ability to see deities. This power extends not only to Buddhist deities, but also to those which are not. According to Buddhism, the world is filled with various kinds of nonphysical beings, which interact with humans and human situations. They are generally not seen owing to the heaviness of people's self-preoccupation and the narrow limits of their perception. Once again, the ability to see the subtle presence that deities represent depends on extraordinary psychological openness and clarity. This power, like the previous, is found recounted throughout Buddhist history, beginning with Śākyamuni Buddha who is said to have had an untrammeled view of nonmaterial beings in the various nonhuman realms. Because deities are often critical elements in human situations, the ability to see and communicate with them gives *lamas* such as the Karmapas ability to act creatively in situations of distress.

Yogic Powers. In the Karmapa biographies, a number of additional abilities are mentioned that are connected intimately with advanced practices of meditation. When Rangjung Dorje sees the universe in his body, this reflects practices of *prāṇa, nāḍī* and *bindu,* wherein the practitioner explores subtle aspects of his psychosomatic being. When Dusum Khyenpa travels to Ceylon to receive teaching from the Mahāsiddha Vajraghaṇṭā, he is practicing the flight of the subtle body, a technique attested to throughout the Indian and Tibetan *vajrayāna.* When Yeshe Dorje emanates many bodies to teach, he is exemplifying the duplication of forms enumerated in the *mahāyāna* as one of the powers of a *bodhisattva.* All of these practices are descriptions of experiences that arise as fruits of long termed and highly developed meditation practice. They are connected with seeing through and abandoning the assumed identification of psychological limit with physical limit. Again, they become possible when self-preoccupation, rigid assumption and firm mental fixation become diminished through meditation.

The Tulku *Phenomenon.* The last primarily psychological ability is the group of powers connected with the *tulku* phenomenon. As is well-known, in Tibetan Buddhism there exist lineages of figures such as the Karmapas who are linked together in one unbroken series of incarnations: when one Karmapa dies, he is reborn shortly thereafter, is discovered through various procedures, and continues the line until he, in turn, dies and is subsequently reborn. Connected with this phenomenon of the *tulku* or reincarnated *lama,* are a whole series of extraordinary abilities. Thus, throughout the Karmapa biographies, *tulkus* speak on the day of their birth, owing to the memory of training in their previous life; they regularly show at an early age sophisticated knowledge of Buddhist theory and practice; they can identify possessions and friends of their previous incarnation; and they possess detailed and accurate memories of their former lives. Such abilities are understood to arise quite naturally out of two causes: first, the identity of the previous and present incarnation; second, the tulku's extraordinary mental clarity which allows previous experience to arise without confusion. Again, this power like the others is not something peculiar to these biographies, but has a long history extending back into Indian Buddhism, to the time of the Buddha himself.

Extraordinary Phenomena Based on the Connection of Mind and External World

Although the preceding "magical" abilities are certainly not familiar parts of our Western experience, because they are all psychological in nature, perhaps the Western reader will be willing to allow for their possibility. Our notions of reality do not *ipso facto* exclude such experiences and, the reader may say, perhaps they are legitimately included in the biographies of the Karmapas. But now we come to a second, much more resistent type of "magical" powers. These are apparently much further removed from our notions of what is possible. These powers have to do with the inherent connection between oneself and the external world, between the way one is and acts and that which occurs in the external world.

The ground of this second type of ability is the Tibetan Buddhist notion that reality, both internal and external, is fundamentally spiritual in nature. This means that the world constantly speaks. The large and small events of one's life, even apparently random accidents and blessings, all have inherent sense and significance. One's sickness and health, the state of one's family and business, the progress of undertakings, even the apparent insignificance of mundane, day to day routines, all have their meaning. What happens in one's life is very much in tune with who one is and what one is doing, from a spiritual viewpoint. On a general level, the more one resists insight, clarity and the insecurity of openness, the more one finds in one's world hellish claustrophobia. Conversely, accepting one's perceptions and intuitions leads to spaciousness and harmony. From the Tibetan viewpoint, reality presents itself as an accurate, apt and timely mirror, and as a challenge, encouragement and critic. One has the opportunity to learn about one's blindness and rigidity from everything that happens.

There are corollaries to this viewpoint. First, the rigid separation that we make in the West between inner and outer, between self and external world, does not hold in the Tibetan view. In fact, self and external reality are two poles of a constant and ongoing dialogue. Second, we are entirely responsible for our world. Everything that arises in our world has to do with us, and we must assume responsibility for it. This holds whether from the conventional moral viewpoint we are held responsible or not. Whatever enters our "life stream," as the Buddhists put it, becomes a manifestation of our life, and we are bound to communicate with it. We cannot reject it as someone else's fault or as an accidental or irrelevant occurrence. Third, we actually affect and bring about our world by who we are and what we do. The more we sink into darkness, ignorance and neurosis, the more we provoke confusion and suffering in our lives. Equally, we can take the opposite tack, and provoke clarity, ease and sanity.

The Tibetans, then, experienced reality as spiritual and this meant that for them, the external world was alive with meaning. Times of spiritual distress and suffering had their physical portents. The birth of a great *lama* or the moment of a spiritual discovery would be accompanied by extraordinary climatic and atmospheric phenomena. In general, the environment was experienced as extraordinarily responsive to the human presence within it. When a high *lama* would appear in a region, his visit might well be heralded by unusual phenomena. His mere presence might affect deleterious situations for the good. And, in times of plague, famine or war, his activity might well change the course of events. Significantly, this activity was carried out not through technology in the Western sense, but through the power of his spirituality. It was experienced that around people of great sanity, the world would literally listen and respond. It is this kind of general logic, further elaborated in various traditional techniques and procedures, that underlies the second type of magical phenomena.

Healing Powers. The Karmapas were well known for their ability to heal sickness and plague, both of individuals and of whole regions. Dusum Khyenpa is remembered for curing disease, blindness and paralysis. Rolpe Dorje and Mikyo Dorje were both able to bring to an end, respectively, smallpox and leprosy epidemics in their times. This healing ability again goes back to the early times of Buddhism, and is recounted in the Buddhist tradition as a constant activity of *buddhas* and *bodhisattvas.* Traditional theory has it that the healer affects the *karmic* stream of stricken individuals by taking their *karma* on himself. This is literally evidenced in their biographies by Mikyo Dorje who himself died of leprosy after curing the leprosy epidemic.

Moving or Affecting Material Objects. Karma Pakshi moved a huge statue through the power of his meditation and Mikyo Dorje left footprints in stone as well as causing a stone carving to speak. This kind of ability to affect material objects is found in Buddhism since the earliest times, and is described in the Pāli Canon most prominently in the *siddhis* or magical powers resulting from meditation. Later during *mahāyāna* times, the *Bodhisattvabhūmi* credits the *bodhisattva* with the power to shake a monastery or even a town, to increase or decrease the size of material objects and to transform the four elements into one another. In the *vajrayāna* tradition of the Karmapas it is said that the *yogin* has power over the four elements. The possibility of such powers is provided by the fact that what people regard as natural limits is based on unquestioned psychological assumptions and fixations rather than on the nature of reality itself.

Divination. Divination is another ability commonly attributed to the Karmapas in this biography. Both Chodrag Gyatsho and Rigpe Dorje make use of it in times of political danger. And Rangjung Dorje discovered the death of the Chinese emperor long before the news reached him. Divination was common throughout Tibetan history, drawing on *vajrayāna* Buddhism, central Asian shamanic practices, and purely indigenous Tibetan traditions, and was carried out through a variety of traditional techniques and methods. Divination is based on the indivisibility of mind and the external world in that the practitioner, through "reading" experiences and ritual objects, can gain knowledge of the larger situation.

Synchronicity. One of the most interesting and also well-documented type of "magical" or miraculous phenomena in Tibetan Buddhism is one we call synchronicity, for want of a better term. It involves all of those environmental and atmospheric phenomena that are so frequently said to accompany *lamas* of high attainment. The best example of this in our biographies occurs during

Dezhin Shegpa's visit to Yung Lo, the emperor of China during the Ming Dynasty. On that occasion, a magical temple appeared in the sky, the clouds took on the shape of *arhats,* the rain was perfumed, lights emanated from Dezhin Shegpa's shrine, and many other similar wonders occurred. The emperor was so impressed that he commissioned a painter to depict them in a mural. Again, this kind of phenomena goes back to the time of Śākyamuni Buddha whose life, it is said, was continually accompanied by such portents and signs. It reappears over and over in the Buddhism of India and Tibet where wonders are said to accompany the births, lives and activities of accomplished people. The logic for this type of event is simple. The universe is fundamentally spiritual in nature and any occurrence of spiritual significance is heralded and celebrated by reality, both animate and inanimate.

Ability to Transform Weather. Rangjung Rigpe Dorje's biography tells us that the present Karmapa visited a monastery in the Nangchen area that was afflicted with a drought. While there, he was requested to bring an end to the drought. In accordance with traditional practice, he asked for water and began to bathe himself, whereupon it began to rain and a spring arose under the washtub he was using. Other similar incidents are recounted elsewhere in the Karmapa biographies and, in general, such abilities are well-known and documented throughout Tibetan Buddhist history. Again, such powers were known in Indian Buddhism: the *mahāyāna bodhisattva* could change earth into water and the *tantric mahāsiddha* had power over the elements. According to Tibetan tradition, rain can be produced by establishing communication with the spiritual presence called *nāgas,* which are connected with the phenomenon of rain.

The above examples and commentary certainly do not "explain" the magical phenomena occurring in the biographies of the Karmapas. What they do suggest is the presuppositions and conditions under which magic comes into question within the Tibetan context. In fact, from what we have said, it should appear questionable whether magic can ever be "explained" in the same way one might explain the operation of, for example, a wrist watch. This is so because, as we have noted, magic in Tibet—in the Buddhist context—was not merely produced by certain activities but was in some sense dependent on psychological and spiritual development.

The conditions under which the magical and miraculous come into play are, to summarize, few and simple. The extraordinary phenomena described in these biographies cannot occur as long as ego, self-preoccupation and conceptual mind hold sway. When, through meditation, one's mind ceases to be filled with thoughts of security, personal territory and self-aggrandizement, then a larger world begins to show itself. This is the world of insight, self-abandonment to other's welfare, and the sacredness of the world, described in the previous section of this introduction. And this is the world where all sorts of extraordinary possibilities can come into view, which we in the West call magic. Egolessness, in the Buddhist sense, is thus a precondition of magic as it is described in these biographies. This being so, such phenomena may perform several functions. They help sentient beings to the health, peace, and welfare they need to develop spiritually. They startle unbelievers with the reality and power of enlightenment. And they set apart, punctuate, and glorify the *lamas* who carry the tradition of Buddhism for their generation. Magic is then, in Tibetan Buddhist tradition, the handmaiden of enlightenment.

Conclusion

For a long time in the study of non-Western religions, it was thought that material such as the present biographies were little more than tales based on mistaken notions about reality. In Western academic theory, stories such as these have frequently been understood to be based on intellectual beliefs with no experiential foundation in actual life. As we have suggested in this introduction, nothing could be further from the case. In fact, as the reader approaches these stories, it is critical that he keeps one fact in mind: the world that opens up in these biographies is a traditional world and a real world. Probably, in some ways less than our "modern world," it was based on superstition, illusion and mental fixation. We say this because of the prominent role played by meditation in Tibetan Buddhism. More than we, the traditional Tibetan masters developed profound self knowledge and aimed to empty themselves of presuppositions and illusion, so that they might see the world freshly and clearly.

We should also keep in mind that the traditional world of the Tibetans, with its visions, its magic and its view of life, was not untested, nor was it fixed and rigid. The variety of techniques, traditions and experiences of the Tibetan Buddhist were continually subjected to the critical and discerning eye of meditation. The various dimensions of Buddhist tradition were explored, tested, confirmed, refined, improved. And this continual evaluation was done by intelligent, educated and sophisticated people. In this way, the profound heart of the tradition and that which was of no-account could be differentiated. Based on the intelligence and experience of the meditative tradition, what was valuable could be retained, what was unnecessary could be discarded, and the tradition could grow, evolve and develop without losing its essential identity.

When we, as Westerners, look at the world of the traditional Tibetan, we are usually first struck by its lack of technological sophistication and its material simplicity. Generally, we tend to dismiss such a traditional world because we see in it a lack of intelligence, open-mindedness or industry. Why else would people like the Tibetans have remained satisfied with their culture, their religion and their way of life? Such thoughts come readily to our minds, but perhaps in them we are self-deceived. In this day and age, we should carefully consider whether there may not be another reason why traditional Tibet remained unchanged for so long. Perhaps within that culture, the Tibetans found a way of life worth keeping and preserving, a way of life which enabled them to some more basic satisfaction. And this suggests that beyond material comfort and security, beyond ease, recognition and fortune, there may be something else more fundamentally needed to make life worth living. Perhaps it was this additional factor that was provided by Tibetan Buddhism—some experience and acceptance of who one actually is, a feeling of contact with reality beyond neurosis and self-absorption, and some experience and appreciation of life in its elemental aspects. Perhaps the Buddhist meditative tradition enabled the Tibetans to live their lives fully, to experience what human life fundamentally is, and to know what it means to be human. Perhaps it is this that lies at the basis of the Tibetans' contentment with their way of life. Before we dismiss these biographies too quickly, we should stop our minds and take such a possibility seriously.

Reginald A. Ray
Naropa Institute
Boulder, Colorado
December, 1979

Śrī Tilopa

The Historical and Theoretical Background

THIS BOOK CONTAINS the biographies of the sixteen successive incarnations of the Gyalwa Karmapa Lama of Tibet, head of the Karma Kagyu lineage of Buddhism. The activity and teaching of this great incarnation line has been of the utmost importance in the history of *vajrayāna* Buddhism to this day.

The present Karmapa, Rangjung Rigpe Dorje (1923–), is the sixteenth of the line which began with the first Karmapa, Dusum Khyenpa (1110–1193). The Gyalwa Karmapa Lamas have continually embodied and guided the Karma Kagyu transmission of the message of Śākyamuni Buddha. They have displayed their mastery of *dharma* variously as scholar, *yogin,* artist and poet and their lives are flawless examples of renunciation, compassion and the view of wisdom.

From the point of view of spirituality, the Karmapa Lamas embody the activity (Skt.: *karma,* Tib.: *phrin.las*)[1] of buddhahood, and as such were prophesied by Śākyamuni Buddha in the *Samādhirājasūtra.* In addition, their activity was also prophesied by the eighth-century Indian *mahāguru,* Padmasambhava.

The Notion of Lineage

The notion of lineage is of the utmost importance for an understanding of the history of the Gyalwa Karmapas. The teachings of Buddha have been preserved for two thousand five hundred years in a multiplicity of lineages. Lord Buddha himself gave many varied and sometimes contrasting instructions to his students, who subsequently specialized in particular cycles of precepts. Out of these early groupings of *dharma* followers emerged the eighteen *hīnayāna* sects. Later the *mahāyāna* traditions of the Madhyamaka and Yogācāra flourished as a result of the inspiration of the two supreme masters, Nāgārjuna and Asaṅga. Subsequently from the fifth century C.E. onward, the various lines of the *vajrayāna* or "secret *mantra*" emerged. Therefore, when the *buddhadharma* was transmitted to Tibet, the Tibetan lineages developed to a large extent on the basis of this pre-existing pattern.

A "lineage" (Tib.: *brgyud*) or "tradition of *dharma*" (Tib.: *chos.lugs*) possesses certain recognizable characteristics, including a central spiritual theme or "viewpoint" (Tib.: *lta.ba*) such as the Kagyu *mahāmudrā*. This view is itself associated with specific practices and symbolic deities. Moreover, the particular teachings are preserved by and passed on through a line of accomplished spiritual masters, who themselves embody the actual qualities of the teaching. The major lineages of *dharma* in Tibet possessed a relatively sophisticated degree of organization, with many monasteries, convents, colleges and meditation centers in which students were trained in a range of studies including philosophy, meditation, ritual, art and astrology.

In addition to the line of transmission from teacher to student within the lineage, there are also the lines of *tulkus* (Tib.: *sprul.sku*) or "incarnate teachers." Incarnate teachers are spiritually advanced practitioners, who, having transcended the network of ego, nevertheless return in successive lives to carry out their vow to work for sentient beings. The second Karmapa, Karma Pakshi was in fact the first recognized Tibetan *tulku*. Although incarnate teachers had been recognized in India, the existence in Tibet of developed traditions with great cultural and social influence enabled *tulkus* to be recognized and trained in a way which had not been possible in India. Within the Tibetan lineages, the incarnate teachers have been regarded as the jewels of the tradition and have generally been the senior teachers, *yogins* and scholars.

In the thousand year history of *buddhadharma* in Tibet four major traditions, Nyingma, Sakya, Gelug and Kagyu have developed. Numerous small lines and sub-sects have also arisen, most of which have since disappeared as independent schools.

The Kagyu Tradition

The Karma Kagyu lineage has been the most extensive of the original four great branches of the Dakpo Kagyu tradition, which is the name given to the systematization of the lineages of teaching transmitted through Gampopa (Tib.: *sgam.po.pa*) (1079–1153), the profound scholar and spiritual master whose life was predicted by Lord Śākyamuni. The Buddha told one of his followers, a physician *bhikṣu* named Kumāra, that in the future he would again be a physician *bhikṣu*, only this time in a northern country by the side of the river Lohita and would establish a meditation school. Gampopa, a skilled physician, was first a Kadampa *bhikṣu* who received teachings from Jayondag, Jayulwa, Geshe Nyugrumpa, Shawo Gangpa and Geshe Chakregongkhapa. He studied the "graded path" (Tib.: *lam.rim*) teachings of Atīśa and the teachings of Dromtonpa. He became a holder of the Kadampa lineage and wrote the *Jewel Ornament of Liberation* and other commentaries on Kadampa teaching. Later he received the Kagyupa teaching on *mahāmudrā* and the "six *yogas* of Nāropa" from Milarepa. After that he was called "two streams become one" (Tib.: *bka'.phyag.chu.bo.gnyis.'dres*). Gampopa organized these lineages into an organic whole, giving his name, Dakpo Lharje (Tib.: *dwags.po.lha.rje*) "the doctor from Dakpo" to the school he formed, which thus became known as the Dakpo Kagyu. After Gampopa's death the "four great and eight minor (sects)" (Tib.: *che.zhi.chung.brgyad*) comprising the Dakpo Kagyu tradition, emerged.

The term Kagyu (Tib.: *bka'.brgyud*) derives from a longer phrase meaning "lineages of the four commissioned ones" (Tib.: *bka'.babs.bzhi'i.brgyud.pa* or sometimes *bka'.bzhi'i.brgyud.pa*). The lineages referred to being: (1) that of Guhyasamāja, Catuḥpīṭha and the *yogas* of the "illusory body" and "transference" handed down through Dharmakāya Buddha Vajradhara, Indrabhūti, Yoginī, Viśukalpa, Saraha, Nāgārjuna and Tilopa; (2) that of Mahāmāyā and the "dream" *yoga* handed down through Dharmakāya Buddha Vajradhara, Jñāna Ḍākinī, Kukuripa, Caryāpa and Tilopa; (3) that of Cakrasaṃvara and the other mother *tantras*, and the "luminosity" *yoga* handed down by Dharmakāya Buddha Vajradhara, Vajrapāṇi, Ḍombipa, Vinasavajra, Lavapa and Tilopa; and finally (4) that of Hevajra and the "heat" *yoga* handed down through Dharmakāya Buddha Vajradhara, Vajrapāṇi, Kāmadevavajra, Padmavajra, Ḍākinī Kalpa Bhadre and Tilopa. The term Kagyu is often translated simply as "oral transmission" but this is only an attempt at literal translation and overlooks the origin of the term and its original meaning. The alternate rendering of the term as Kargyu (Tib.: *dkar.brgyud*) is a late Drukpa Kagyu custom referring to the wearing of a "white" (Tib.: *dkar*) cotton robe by the *yogins* of the tradition.

Gampopa's principal teacher, the famed *yogin* and poet, Milarepa, had himself received the "transmission" of the lineage from Marpa the translator, student of Nāropa and Maitrīpa. He thus became the holder of the Kagyu lineage. The "direct lineage" (Tib.: *nye.brgyud*) of the Dakpo Kagyu is described as:

Dharmakāya Buddha Vajradhara
Tilopa
Nāropa
Marpa Lotsawa
Milarepa
Gampopa

The "indirect lineage" (Tib.: *ring.brgyud*), which is expressly concerned with the transmission of *mahāmudrā*, is described as:

Dharmakāya Buddha Vajradhara
Ratnamati
Saraha
Nāgārjuna
Śavaripa
Maitrīpa
(Ratnamati through Maitrīpa: Indian *siddhas*)
Marpa Lotsawa
Milarepa
Gampopa

The "four great" (Tib.: *che.bzhi*) lineages of the Dakpo Kagyu originated with pupils of Gampopa or his nephew, Dakpo Gomtsul (1116–1169): (1) The Kaṃtshang or Karma Kagyu was founded by Karmapa Dusum Khyenpa (1110–1193), who studied under Gampopa. (2) The Tsalpa (Tib.: *tshal.pa*) Kagyu was founded by Zhang Yudrakpa Tsondru Drakpa (1123–1193), a disciple of Dakpo Gomtsul. (3) The Baram (Tib.: *'ba'.ram*) Kagyu was founded by Baram Darma Wangchuk, a disciple of Gampopa. (4) The Phagmo Drupa (Tib.: *phag.mo.gru.pa*) Kagyu was founded by Gampopa's student, Phagmo Dru Dorje Gyalpo (1110–1170). The Phagmo Drupa Kagyu subsequently spawned "eight minor" (Tib.: *chung.brgyad*) subsects:

Drigung	(Tib.: *'bri.gung*)
Taglung	(Tib.: *stag.lung*)
Trophu	(Tib.: *khro.phu*)
Drukpa	(Tib.: *'brug.pa*)
Martshang	(Tib.: *smar.tshang*)
Yelpa	(Tib.: *gyel.pa*)
Shugseb	(Tib.: *shug.seb*)
Yamzang	(Tib.: *gya'.zang*)

The Drukpa, Drigung and Taglung have survived to the present day, with the Drukpa being the largest, followed by the Drigung.

The Other Lineages

The Karma Kagyu tradition cannot be considered in isolation from the other traditions of Buddhism in Tibet upon which it exerted considerable influence and from which, in return, it received many teachings. The first tradition to appear in Tibet was the Nyingma (Tib.: *rnying.ma*) or "Ancient Ones," which emerged out of the missionary work of the eighth-century masters, Guru Padmasambhava, King Trisong Detsun and the *bodhisattva* Śāntarakshita. The early Nyingmapas were both lay and monastic practitioners who followed the *sūtra* and *mantra* teachings of the period of early translations. The key Nyingma precept is *mahā ati* (Tib.: *rdzogs.pa.chen.po*) or "Great Perfection," which was introduced into Tibet in the eighth century by the Indian scholar and *yogin,* Vimalamitra. The teaching of *mahā ati* points directly to the natural perfection of awareness, and it may be regarded as the supreme teaching of the Buddha's way. The main *tantra* of the Nyingma tradition is the *Guhyagarbha* (Tib.: *gsang.ba.snying.po*) or *Secret Essence.* Three distinct lines can be distinguished within the Nyingma school: the "indirect lineage" (Tib.: *ring.brgyud*) of the "oral transmission" (Tib.: *bka'.ma*), the "direct lineage" (Tib.: *nye.brgyud*) of "the treasures" or "concealed texts" (Tib.: *gter.ma*) and the lineage of "profound visions" (Tib.: *zab.mo.dag.snang*). The greatest masters of the Nyingma tradition included the omniscient Longchen Rabjampa (1308–1363), Jigme Lingpa (1729–1797) and Ju Mipham (1848–1914). The present heads of the Nyingma school are Minling Trichen and Dudjom Jigdral Yeshe Dorje.

The later schools in Tibet collectively belong to the period of the "new translations" (Tib.: *nga.'gyur.gsar.ma*), which began in the tenth century when Rinchen Zangpo (958–1051) and other scholars devised new canons of translation technique, emphasizing etymological precision rather than the freer style of the "old translation" school. The Sakya and Kagyu traditions, both of which arose in the eleventh century, were based on the "new" *tantric* cycles which were introduced at this time.

The monastery of Sakya, which later became the central seat of the Sakyapa (Tib.: *sa.skya.pa*) school, was founded in 1073 by Konchog Gyalpo of the Khon family. This influential family had previously been Nyingmapa but Konchog Gyalpo studied the new *tantras* with Drogmi Lotsawa and the Indian *paṇḍita,* Gayadhara. The Sakya tradition was given definite shape by Konchog Gyalpo's son, Sachen Kunga Nyingpo (1092-1158) and the other four of the "five great masters," Sonam Tsemo (1142–1182), Jetsun Drakpa Gyaltsen (1147–1216), Sakya Paṇḍita (1182–1251) and Chogyal Phakpa (1235–1280).

The Sakya school has specialized in the combined *sūtra* and *mantra* teaching of the *lam dre* (Tib.: *lam.'bras*) or "path and fruit" cycle, developed by the Indian *siddha*, Virūpa. Their principal Sakya *tantra* has been *Hevajra* and their main deities are Hevajra and Vajrayoginī. Three sub-sects have appeared: Sakyapa, Ngorpa and Tsharpa, which, however, have differed only in ritual. The present head of the Sakya tradition is H. H. Sakya Tridzin (1945–), an emanation of Mañjuśrī, the *bodhisattva* of wisdom.

The Kadampa (Tib.: *bka'.gdams.pa*) tradition also began in the eleventh century but it has not survived as an independent school, its teaching having been absorbed into the other schools. The Kadam school developed from the activity and teachings of the Indian master Atīśa Dīpaṅkara Śrījñāna (979–1053), who spent the last twelve years of his life in Tibet. Atīśa laid great emphasis on the "graded path" of both *sūtra* and *tantra* as an essential prerequisite for authentic spirituality. To a few gifted disciples he transmitted the especially profound precepts of "thought transformation" (Tib.: *blo.sbyong*).

It was his student Dromton (Tib.: *'brom.ston.rgyal.ba'i.byung.nas*) who actually organized the Kadam as a school. The Kadampas generally upheld the philosophy of the Prāsaṅgika Madhyamaka teaching of "emptiness" (Skt.: *śūnyatā*, Tib.: *stong.pa.nyid*) as a negation of all predicates.

The Gelug tradition was founded by the great Tibetan *paṇḍita* Tsongkhapa Lozang Dragpa (Tib.: *tsong.kha.pa.blo.bzang.'grags.pa*) (1367–1419). In early life Tsongkhapa studied with masters of all the major lineages and displayed superb qualities of scholarship. He gathered many disciples and out of them grew the Gelug tradition. The central concerns of the Gelug tradition are its insistence on the *vinaya* monastic rules and the "graded path" to enlightenment inherited from Atīśa's teachings. This emphasis on the teachings of Atīśa has led to the Gelug sometimes being referred to as the new Kadam (Tib.: *bka'.gdams.sar*). Their particular philosophical viewpoint is that of the Prāsaṅgika Madhyamaka as elaborated by Tsongkhapa. In *tantra*, they have placed their main emphasis on the *tantras* of Guhyasamāja, Vajrabhairava and Cakrasaṃvara. The Gelugpa tradition has been ornamented by the work of many brilliant scholars such as Khedrupje (Tib.: *mkhas.grub.rje*) (1385–1438) and Konchog Jigme Wangpo (Tib.: *dkon.chog.'jigs.med.dbang.po*) (1728–1781). The present head of the school is H. H. Ling Rinpoche, tutor to the fourteenth Dalai Lama, Tenzin Gyatsho (1935–), embodiment of the compassion of Avalokiteśvara.

In addition to these major traditions a great contribution to *buddhadharma* in Tibet has been made by the various smaller lineages. Important ones include the Shijay (Tib.: *shi.byas*) and Chod Yul (Tib.: *gcod.yul*) lineages of the Indian *siddha,* Dampa Sangye (Tib.: *dams.pa.sangs.rgyas*) and his student, the famed *yoginī,* Machig Labdronma (Tib.: *ma.gcig.labs. sgron.ma*) (1055–1145); the Urgyen Nyendrup (Tib.: *o.rgyan.snyen.sgrub*) lineage of the *siddha,* Urgyenpa Rinchen Pal (Tib.: *u.rgyan.pa.rin.chen. dpal*) (1230–1309), which was very influential for the Drugpa and Kaṃtshang Kagyu lineages into which it was eventually absorbed; and the Shangpa (Tib.: *shangs.pa*), founded by Khyungpo Naljor (Tib.: *khyung. po.rnal.'byor*) (990–1140), who inherited the *mahāmudrā* transmission of the *ḍākinīs,* Niguma (consort of Nāropa) and Sukhasiddhi.

One of the most controversial sects in Tibet was the Jonang school (Tib.: *jo.nang.pa*) founded by the learned philosopher, Dolpopa Sherab Gyaltshan (Tib.: *dol.po.pa.shes.rab.rgyal.mtshan*) (1292-1361). The Jonang tradition held the influential doctrine of "empty of something else" (Tib.: *gzhan.stong*). This view, which is derived from the *Uttaratantra* (Tib.: *rgyud.bla.ma*) of Maitreya, states that ultimate reality, while being empty of any relative blemishes, is intrinsically positive. The Jonangpas subsequently were attacked by many Prāsaṅgika scholars, especially the Gelugpas at the time of the fifth Dalai Lama (1615–1680) and since this time have not existed as an independent sect. However, their teachings have been maintained and propagated by certain figures within the Kagyu, Nyingma and Sakya traditions, such as Karmapa Rangjung Dorje, Longchenpa and Śākya Chokden.

The Lineage of the Karmapas

The Karma Kagyu school has had a long and glorious history in which it has established itself as the supreme Kagyu sect under the leadership of the Gyalwa Karmapas. It has spread from Ladakh to China, and now to the West. The Black Hat (Tib.: *zhwa.nag*) line of the Karmapas has been aided and supported by the three chief incarnation lines of the sect: the Red Hat Shamar (Tib.: *zhwa.dmar*), Situ (Tib.: *si.tu*) and Gyaltshab (Tib.: *rgyal. tshab*) *tulkus.* In addition, numerous other scholars, *yogins* and visionaries have contributed to the splendor of the tradition. Notable among these have been the Jamgon Kongtrul (Tib.: *'jam.mgon.kong.sprul*), and Pawo (Tib.: *dpa'.bo*) *tulkus.*

The Kaṃtshang Kagyu tradition was established by the first Karmapa, Dusum Khyenpa, who inherited the Kagyu transmission from Gampopa. After he attained enlightenment he was recognized by eminent contemporaries to be "the Man of Buddha Activity" (Tib.: *karma.pa*) prophesied by the Buddha in the *Samādhirājasūtra,* and also to be an embodiment of Avalokiteśvara, the compassionate form of buddhahood. Dusum Khyenpa later founded the three main centers of Karma Kagyu tradition at Todlung Tsurphu (Tib.: *stod.lung.mtshur.phu*) near Lhasa, Karma Gon (Tib.: *karma.dgon*) in Kham province and Kampo Nenang (Tib.: *kam.po.gnas.nang*) also in Kham, and thus organized the Karma Kagyu as a distinct school.

It was during the lifetime of the second Karmapa, Karma Pakshi (1204–1283) that the expansion of the Kaṃtshang began. Famed as a *siddha,* Karma Pakshi was invited to Mongolia by Prince Kublai where he became guru to Mongka Khan and subsequently, though not without initial problems, to his successor, Kublai Khan. While in China, Karma Pakshi on several occasions displayed miraculous powers in order to assist his work of spreading *buddhadharma.* The display of miraculous activity by Karma Pakshi and the other Karmapas has functioned as a means of manifesting the utter freedom of enlightenment. Being beyond the limitations of dualistic perception, such enlightened activity takes on the garb of miraculous power. Its apparently miraculous nature derives from its absolutely spontaneous response to the needs of beings and the particular situation which it confronts.

The third Karmapa, Rangjung Dorje (1284–1339), who was a consummate master of theory and practice is particularly important for his bringing together of the hitherto separate streams of Kagyu *mahāmudrā* and Nyingma *mahā ati.* He received the teachings of the "innermost essence" (Tib.: *snying.gi.thig.le*) of *mahā ati* from Rigdzin Kumārarāja (1266–1343), who was also the guru of Longchenpa. In addition Rangjung Dorje composed the extremely important and influential texts *Zabmo Nangdon* (Tib.: *zab.mo.snang.don*), which dealt with the subtle teachings of the *anuttarayoga tantra.*

Like his two predecessors and his successors up to the tenth Karmapa, the fifth Karmapa Dezhin Shegpa (1384–1415) was the guru of the emperor of China. During one particular ceremony performed by Dezhin Shegpa, the Emperor Yung Lo perceived the spiritual form of the black *vajra* crown above Karmapa's head. The *vajra* crown, which is the symbol of Avalokiteśvara's compassion, is present above the heads of all Karmapa incarnations. The first Karmapa, Dusum Khyenpa, had been presented with the crown by *ḍākinīs* at the moment of his attainment of enlightenment. The spiritual form of the crown was said to be woven from the hair of one hundred thousand *ḍākinīs*. When, through his devotion to Dezhin Shegpa, Yung Lo perceived the *vajra* crown, he determined to have a replica made, ornamented with precious jewels and gold, so that all might be inspired to see the true nature of Karmapa's spirituality. On his receipt of Yung Lo's replica, Dezhin Shegpa developed the ceremony wherein he wore the *vajra* crown while embodying the compassion of Avalokiteśvara. All succeeding Karmapas have followed this custom and the ceremony, which has the power of communicating the unending inspiration of the Karmapa lineage, has become one of the most sacred and characteristic features of the activity of the Karmapas.

The eighth Karmapa, Mikyo Dorje (1507–1554), was a brilliant scholar and prolific author. He composed over thirty texts, including works on *abhidharma* psychology, Madhyamaka philosophy, the *Prajñāpāramitā*, the *vinaya*, logic, *mahāmudrā*, *tantras*, Sanskrit grammar, art and poetry.

During the lifetime of the tenth Karmapa, Choying Dorje (1604–1674), the Karma Kagyu lineage was drawn inevitably into politics[2] because of the antipathy to the Gelugpa sect felt by influential lay supporters such as Desi Karma Tenkyong (Tib.: *de.srid.karma.bstan.skong*), the king of Tsang (Tib.: *gtsang*) province at the time of Choying Dorje.

The fourteenth Karmapa, Thegchog Dorje (1798–1868), played a major role in the nineteenth-century religious and cultural renaissance associated with the Rime (Tib.: *ris.med*) ("boundaryless") movement. His students included the three principal Rime figures: Chogyur Dechen Lingpa (Tib.: *mchog.'gyur.bde.chen.gling.pa*) (1829–1870), Jamyang Khyentse Wangpo (Tib.: *'jam.dbyangs.mkhyen.brtse.dbang.po*) (1820–1892) and Jamgon Kongtrul Lodro Thaye (Tib.: *'jam.mgon.kong.sprul.blo.gros.mtha'.yas*) (1811–1899).

The present Karmapa, Rangjung Rigpe Dorje (1923–) is the sixteenth of the line. His Holiness has presided over the Karma Kagyu school during this period of great change both for the school itself and also for Tibet as a whole. Trained by the leading masters of the Kagyu and other traditions, His Holiness has manifested the tremendous qualities of compassion and natural wisdom of the Gyalwa Karmapas. After the abolition of Buddhist culture in Tibet in 1959, His Holiness brought his followers into exile in Sikkim where he established a new monastic seat at Rumtek. His Holiness has striven unceasingly to maintain the lamp of Kagyu *dharma* and in recent years has twice visited the West at the invitation of his own emissary disciples. Under the enlightened inspiration of this, the sixteenth Gyalwa

Karmapa, the Karma Kagyu tradition is now establishing itself throughout the world.

The Teaching of the Karma Kagyu Tradition

The essential theme of Kagyu teaching is *mahāmudrā,* the realization of the true nature of mind and its radiation in wisdom and compassion. It is the foundation, path and goal of spirituality. Dingo Khyentse Rinpoche compared *mahāmudrā* to a king who affixes his seal to documents and so forth to signify his confirmation. Similarly, the *mahāmudrā* ("great seal") *yogin* realizes that as "buddha-nature" (Skt.: *tathāgatagarbha,* Tib.: *de. gsheg.snying.po*) is the underlying reality of all phenomena, whatever arises is "sealed" (Skt.: *mudrā*) with "coemergent" (Skt.: *sahaja,* Tib.: *lhan.gcig. skyes.pa*) perfection.

The actual instructions and methods of the Kagyu spiritual path derive from Gampopa's unification of the Kadam "graded path" *dharma* and the *tantric* precepts of the *mahāsiddhas.* Its chief philosophical base is the *Uttaratantra* of Maitreya and its commentary by Asaṅga. The *mahāmudrā* theme embraces all the apparent multiplicity of these precepts and practices.

Within *saṃsāra,* as sentient beings are alienated from the true nature of reality, "buddha-nature" exists only as an indwelling potential obscured by unawareness and various defilements (Skt.: *kleśa*). The spiritual path is the liberation of "buddha-nature" and its fulfillment as *dharmakāya.* As Gampopa says in *The Jewel Ornament of Liberation,* "The motive is buddha-nature." This transforming path has three main stages or "vehicles" (Skt.: *yāna,* Tib.: *theg.pa*) of development: *hīnayāna, mahāyāna* and *vajrayāna. Mahāmudrā* is itself the crown or climax of the path.

Hīnayāna

The starting point of the spiritual path is the *hīnayāna* ("narrow vehicle") way. In its exclusive approach the *hīnayāna* focuses on the frustration that permeates all aspects of our experience, due to clinging to the illusory notion of a permanent, independent self. This recognition derives from Buddha's enunciation of the "four truths": (1) suffering, (2) its cause, self-clinging, (3) liberation, (4) its cause, the eightfold path of right view, intention, action, speech, livelihood, effort, mindfulness and meditative concentration. This teaching provides a diagnosis of our illness and its cause and the prescription of the method of attaining health. By applying the simple precision and dignity of the *hīnayāna* in meditation and everyday life the practitioner develops an understanding that conditioned reality is impermanent, sorrowful and egoless. From this understanding comes a natural, unfeigned renunciation. This is the key concept of the *hīnayāna* path.

Within the Kagyu tradition a series of precepts known as "the four thoughts that turn the mind (to *dharma*)" (Tib.: *blo.ldog.nam.bzhi*) are utilized as a particularly effective means of realizing the "four truths." The four thoughts are: (1) precious human life (Tib.: *mi.lus.rin.po.che*), (2) death and impermanence (Tib.: *'chi.ba.mi.rtags.pa*), (3) action and result (Tib.: *las.'bras*), (4) defects of *saṃsāra* (Tib.: *'khor.ba'i.nyes.pa*). They have been inherited from the tradition of Atīśa and elaborated by Gampopa and successive Kagyu masters.

The first thought is the reflection on the uniquely positive situation of precious human life with its freedom and ability. Within the varied forms of embodied life, human birth, which is free from situations of entrapment and limitations, is extremely rare. In addition, human life becomes precious through contact with the *buddhadharma.* Such unique "opportunity" and "juncture" (Tib.: *dal.'byor*) constitute precious human life, the sole basis of spiritual endeavor.

The second thought is the reflection on the impermanence of all phenomena. As Buddha has said, "the end of every meeting is parting." Ego derives its sense of security from the notion of its own permanence and that of its relationships and possessions. Realization of impermanence in meditation and everyday life cuts through the laziness and self-satisfaction of neurotic mind and prepares the practitioner for evolution on the path.

Thirdly comes the reflection on actions and results. Past actions by body, speech and mind have brought about the particular characteristics of the present. The present situation itself provides a variety of choices for action out of which the future situation will develop. Generally action is divided into the three categories of virtuous, nonvirtuous and neutral, which have their corresponding results in positive, negative or neutral situations and environments. This third thought thus enables the practitioner to acknowledge responsibility for all aspects of his life and develop a spaciousness of mind suitable for spiritual growth.

The fourth and final thought is the reflection on the defects of *saṃsāra.* All sentient beings are trapped within the sufferings of conditioned existence. *Saṃsāra* is variously hostile, fascinating and bewildering but in it there is no ultimate satisfaction or security for ego. Understanding of this produces a true turning away from *saṃsāra* and a longing for the path of liberation, symbolized by the three jewels of *buddha, dharma* and *saṅgha.*

Mahāyāna

As the practice of *hīnayāna* brings about a detachment from the fixation on ego, a natural spaciousness and openness develops. This is the dawn of the *mahāyāna* path. Its key concept is *bodhicitta,* the union of *prajñā* and compassion which arises out of the all-encompassing space of "buddha-nature." Its *prajñā* consists in its direct penetration of the "emptiness" of ego and phenomena. Its compassion consists in its responsiveness to the needs of others.

Within our tradition many precepts exist for both relative and ultimate *bodhicitta.* In particular we have inherited precepts of relative *bodhicitta* from the Kadam school, such as the famous "seven stages of thought transformation" (Tib.: *blo.sbyong.don.bdun.ma*) through which one develops the fearlessness of *bodhicitta* in exchanging oneself for another.

Ultimate *bodhicitta* practice is meditation on "emptiness," in which the practitioner sees the space-like "emptiness" of reality, free from the extremes of existence and nonexistence. From the Madhyamaka teachings, of *paṇḍita* Nāgārjuna and the teachings of the *siddhas,* Gampopa brought together many precepts for ultimate *bodhicitta* meditation. He termed this approach "*sūtra* tradition *mahāmudrā*" (Tib.: *mdo.lugs.phyag.rgya.chen.po*).

The all-powerful inspiration of *bodhicitta* extends outward into all aspects of life as the activity of the six "perfections" (Skt.: *pāramitā,* Tib.: *pha.rol.tu.phyin.pa*): giving, morality, patience, energy, meditation and *prajñā.*

Vajrayāna

The *vajrayāna* or *tantrayāna* is the highest level of Buddha's way. In the lower *yānas* the practitioner follows a path which will lead to enlightenment in the future. However, in the *vajrayāna* the practitioner adopts the goal itself as the path. The spaciousness of *mahāyāna* gives birth to the *vajrayāna* perception of the universe as the play of interwoven Buddha-energies, so at the level of *tantra,* body, speech and mind are transformed into the body, speech and mind of buddha. The key concept of *vajrayāna* is *samaya,* which is the *yogin's* commitment to the perfect purity of the *vajrayāna* vision.

In *vajrayāna,* buddahood is directly manifested in the "three roots" (Tib.: *rtsa.ba.gsum*) of *guru* (Tib.: *bla.ma*), *devatā* (Tib.: *yi.dam*) and *ḍākinī* (Tib.: *mkha'.gro*) and *dharmapāla* (Tib.: *chos.skyong*), which are, in effect, the *tantric* aspect of the three jewels. The *guru* is the root of "inspiration" (Skt.: *adhiṣṭhāna,* Tib.: *sbyin.brlabs*) as he is the one who reveals the presence of the Buddha within our mind. The *devatā* ("deity") is the root of "attainment" (Skt.: *siddhi,* Tib.: *dngos.grub*), as buddhahood manifests in a multiplicity of forms to benefit different aptitudes and dispositions. So the *yogin* performs the spiritual practice of the deity or deities which embody the awakened transformation of his own particular disposition. The *ḍākinīs* ("sky-goers") and *dharmapālas* ("dharma-protectors") together comprise the root of "activity" (Skt.: *karma,* Tib.: *phrin. las*). The *ḍākinīs* embody the feminine energy of enlightenment as it appears in situations to guide and restore the *yogin* to a sense of balance. The *dharmapālas,* both male and female aspects, function in an analogous manner to guard the *yogin's* spiritual development and the accumulated blessings of the various lineages of *buddhadharma.*

In our tradition the principal guru is Gyalwa Karmapa, who is inseparable from Vajradhara. The principal *devatā* is Vajravārāhī (Tib.: *rdo. rje.phag.mo*), mother of all Buddhas, and the principal *dharmapālas* are the Vajra Black-Cloaked Mahākāla (Tib.: *gon.po.rdo.rje.ber.nag.can*) and Mahākālī, the Self-Arisen Queen (Tib.: *rang.'byung.rgyal.mo*).

As the practice of *tantra* revolves around the transformation of body, speech and mind into the three *kāyas* of buddhahood, *dharmakāya, sambhogakāya* and *nirmāṇakāya,* the *tantras* include practices relating to each of these three aspects. Bodily practices include prostrations, offerings, walking meditations and yogic postures. Speech practice revolves around *mantra* and liturgy. Mind practice involves visualization in which the dualistic perception of subject and object is purified by the creation of the *devatā* and his environment. Its other aspect is formless meditation, which is *mahāmudrā* meditation.

In the Kagyu, Gelug and Sakya schools, which collectively belong to the "new *tantra*" tradition, there are four orders of *tantra,* whereas in the "old tradition" (Tib.: *rnying.ma*) there are six. The four orders are respectively *kriyā, upa (caryā), yoga* and *anuttarayoga.* The various cycles of *tantras,* commentaries and *sādhanas* are assigned to the appropriate one of these four orders, in respect of their level of spiritual power.

The *kriyā tantra* is the initial stage of *vajrayāna* wherein the emphasis lies on the external, awe-inspiring purity of buddha-energy. The *yogin* relates to the deity as a servant to a master and pays great attention to ritual activity and purity. Avalokiteśvara is an example of a *kriyā tantra* deity.

The second order of *tantra* is *upa* or *caryā.* Here the *yogin* perceives the buddha-energy as both external and internal. This is comparable to the relation between friends. Less stress is placed upon ritual activity at this level. An example of an *upa tantra* deity is Vairocana.

Yoga tantra is the culmination of the *kriyā* and *upa tantras.* Here the *yogin* is consubstantiated with the buddha-energy, so he meditates on himself as identical with the deity. Ritual activity is only little emphasized. The cycle of *Sarvavid* (Tib.: *kun.rig*) is an example of a *yoga tantra.*

The highest order of *tantra* is the *anuttarayoga,* which is radically distinct from the three lower orders in its emphasis on the unsurpassable, all-pervading nature of buddha-energy. *Anuttarayoga* is divided into a "development" (Tib.: *bskye.rim*) and "fulfillment" stage (Tib.: *rdzogs.rim*). In the first stage the *yogin* identifies himself and his environment with the divine appearance of the *devatā* and his palace. The fulfillment stage completes the transformation and itself possesses a twofold aspect, one based on form and one on formlessness. The former aspect is the yoga of the "channels" (Skt.: *nāḍi,* Tib.: *rtsa*), "breath" (Skt.: *prāṇa,* Tib.: *rlung*) and "seed" (Skt.: *bindu,* Tib.: *thig.le*). The latter aspect is meditation on the "coincident luminosity and emptiness" (Tib.: *gsal.stong.zung.'jug*) of natural awareness.

In the Kagyu tradition the principal *anuttarayoga* deities are Vajravārāhī and the group of "five deities" (Tib.: *lha.lnga*): Cakrasaṃvara, Vajrabhairava, Hevajra, Mahāmāyā and Guhyasamāja. These five constitute the fivefold *heruka maṇḍala* of *anuttarayoga.* Vajravārāhī is herself both the mother and consort of all the *herukas.*

Mahāmudrā

Mahāmudrā is simultaneously the climax of *vajrayāna* and the thread running through the entire Kagyu spiritual path. Although essentially it eludes formulation, one may consider that it possesses three aspects: view

(Tib.: *lta.ba*), meditation (Tib.: *bsgom.pa*) and action (Tib.: *spyod.pa*). However, even these three categories are only apparent distinctions as in fact they spring from the unity of the *mahāmudrā* realization.

View. The true nature of mind is the primordial union of "luminosity" and "emptiness." As such it is unborn and undying. However, through the spontaneous arising of unawareness, natural purity becomes obscured and the pattern of *saṃsāra* with its five defilements, five *skandhas* and so on, emerges. Nevertheless the underlying reality of both *saṃsāra* and *nirvāṇa* is the thread of mind's primordial purity, which is termed "buddha-nature." As the great *siddha* Saraha says in his *People Dohās,* "Mind itself is the one seed of everything. From it the world of becoming and *nirvāṇa* arise."

In the vast open nature of this view whatever arises is self-liberated since whatever arises is sealed with "coemergence." The apparent duality of subject and object is reconciled in the unborn and undying nature of awareness. The *dharmatā* of mind is the middle way between the extremes of assertion and negation. As Tilopa declares, "*mahāmudrā* mind dwells nowhere." All phenomena arise and fade in the space of mind, which itself is naturally empty.

Meditation. The heart of *mahāmudrā* is the effortless, uncontrived experience of mind. When the cloud-like obscurations are dispersed, the unborn and undying *dharmakāya* is revealed. Karmapa Rangjung Dorje says,

> The ground of purification is the coincident luminosity and emptiness.
> The purifier is the *vajra yoga* of *mahāmudrā.*
> The purified are the momentary delusions and impurities.
> May the purified fruit of the immaculate *dharmakāya* be realized.

This ultimate realization is generally attained, unless one is especially gifted, as the outcome of the training in both ordinary (Tib.: *thun.mong*) and extraordinary (Tib.: *thun.mong.ma.yin.pa*) *mahāmudrā.*

As with all cycles of teaching, to begin *mahāmudrā* practice the *yogin* must receive the appropriate empowerments (Tib.: *dbang*), textual transmissions (Tib.: *lung*) and instructions (Tib.: *khrid*) from the *guru.* In particular the practitioner must receive the fourth empowerment known as the "awareness empowerment" in which the meeting of the two minds of the *guru* and student takes place and the nature of mind is clearly pointed out.

The preparation for both the ordinary and extraordinary *mahāmudrā* is the practice of the four preliminaries (Tib.: *sngon.'gro*). The four sections of the preliminaries are: (1) refuge and *bodhicitta* combined with prostrations, (2) Vajrasattva meditations and recitation, (3) *maṇḍala* offerings, (4) *guru yoga.* By the accomplishment of each section one hundred thousand times, the practitioner is ripened for the main practice.

In the Karma Kagyu, *guru yogas,* particularly of the eighth Karmapa, Mikyo Dorje, and the second Karmapa, Karma Pakshi, are performed to receive the particular inspiration of the Karmapa lineage.

The ordinary practice of *mahāmudrā* is actually formless meditation itself. In the first stage of tranquillity (Tib.: *zhi.gnas*) the practitioner rests in effortless one-pointedness of mind. When this tranquillity is achieved the *guru* introduces the student to the nature of his own mind (Tib.: *ngo.bo. sprod.pa*). Insight arises wherein the nature of awareness is revealed as nondual "luminosity and emptiness." Thought is the body of *dharmakāya* itself. This is the ultimate realization of *mahāmudrā.*

The extraordinary practice of *mahāmudrā* is comprised of the various "development-stage" meditations such as Vajrayoginī and Cakrasaṃvara and the ensuing "fulfillment-stage" *yogas* such as the "six doctrines of Nāropa" (Tib.: *naro.chos.drug*): inner heat (Tib.: *gtum.mo*), illusory body (Tib.: *sgyu.ma.lus*), dream (Tib.: *mi.lam*), luminosity (Tib.: *'od.gsal*), transference (Tib.: *'pho.ba*) and intermediate state (Tib.: *bar.do*). Their accomplishment leads to the production of the union of "bliss and emptiness" (Tib.: *bde.stong.zung.'jug*), from which the *mahāmudrā* realization spontaneously develops.

Action. The characteristic feature of *mahāmudrā* action is effortlessness. As it results from the complete emptiness and compassion of the view and meditation, it goes beyond the notion of an imposed discipline. Hence the *mahāmudrā yogin* may sometimes behave in a way which is apparently shocking. This kind of action is referred to as the behavior of the "crazy *yogin*" (Tib.: *smyon.pa*). Saraha says,

> If I am like a pig
> That covets worldly mire
> Tell me what fault
> Lies in a stainless mind.

The practice of *chod* (Tib.: *gchod.,* "cutting off ego") is associated with the action of the Kagyu *yogin.* It emphasizes direct openness to both internal and external hindrances. *Chod* entered the Kagyu tradition from the lineage of the eleventh century *yoginī,* Machig Labdronma, and has been propagated by the Karmapa lineage, especially the third, Rangjung Dorje, and Surmang Trungpa Kunga Namgyal.

As one studies these biographies of the Gyalwa Karmapas it is vital to realize their true significance. They are not merely historical accounts but also spiritual doctrines. Essentially they are the records of the liberation (Tib.: *rnam.pa.thar.pa*) of the Karmapa lineage. Their multifaceted quality reflects the equally many-sided nature of *buddhadharma* itself, comprised of the three *yānas* with their multiplicity of spiritual instructions.

The aspects of the biographies which relate the actual history of the Karmapa lineage together with their example as accomplished students and practitioners may be characterized as their *hīnayāna* aspect. In the *hīnayāna* the student grounds himself in the basic truths of *dharma,* thus building a foundation for spiritual development. All the Gyalwa Karmapas have displayed great assiduity in meditation practice and scholarly study. It is said of the first Karmapa, Dusum Khyenpa, that while in meditation retreat, he never unfolded his hands long enough for the sweat on them to dry.

The particular features of the biographies which deal with the compassionate activity of the Karmapas may be considered as their *mahāyāna* aspect. In the *mahāyāna* the student radiates a warmth and openness emanating from the absence of emphasis on self. As the biographies show, each of the Gyalwa Karmapas has worked unceasingly for sentient beings by teaching, healing and establishing the Karma Kagyu lineage itself. This compassionate activity has not been confined merely to practitioners but also extended to the ordinary people of Tibet, China, Mongolia and so on. Like the other Gyalwa Karmapas, Mikyo Dorje did not remain constantly at the monastery of Tsurphu, but journeyed throughout Tibet with his monastic camp and gave teachings and aid to all who requested it. While traveling, Mikyo Dorje composed many texts in which he set forth his profound understanding of *dharma.* His death came as a result of clearing an epidemic of leprosy, which he subsequently contracted himself.

The *vajrayāna* aspects of the biographies may be seen as the varied accounts of visions and miracles. In the *vajrayāna* the practitioner experiences and acts from the standpoint of primordially pure energy of enlightenment itself. As the network of conceptualization is totally transcended, it is the level of visions and miraculous activity. As we see from the biographies, the successive Gyalwa Karmapas have rediscovered their own natural spirituality largely through visionary experience. Furthermore, each has had affinities with particular symbolic deities through which agency they have received visionary inspiration. One famous example of this process is the vision of the third Karmapa, Rangjung Dorje, in which he envisaged that the eighth-century *ati yoga* master Vimalamitra was absorbed into his forehead. As a result of this, Rangjung Dorje unified the two streams of *ati yoga* and *mahāmudrā.*

In this history the underlying clarity and intelligence of the biographies have been stressed. In the presentation of Buddhism in the West the two extremes of arrogant dismissal or over-sentimental naivete have too often obscured the actual nature of the material. In contrast here is a clear and profound account of the lives of the Gyalwa Karmapas, from a representative of the Karma Kagyu tradition, the fourth Karma Thinley *tulku.*

Karma Thinley, Rinpoche was born in Nangchen in Kham in 1931 and was recognized, at the age of two and a half years, by Sakya Tridzin, Dakshul Thinle Rinchen as *tulku* of Beru Shaiyak Lama Kunrik, thought to be a Vairocana incarnation. At that time he received all the symbols and titles of his rank and authority. He was subsequently recognized by His Holiness the sixteenth Gyalwa Karmapa as the fourth Karma Thinleypa. Rinpoche studied with many leading contemporary teachers including Zechen Kongtrul and Dingo Khyentse, Rinpoche, and Ling Rinpoche. In addition to his position as a master of the Kagyu and Sakya schools, Rinpoche is also widely learned in the Nyingma and Gelug traditions. In 1974, His Holiness the Gyalwa Karmapa appointed him a "Lord of Dharma" of the Karma Kagyu lineage. As a leading scholar and close disciple of His Holiness, Rinpoche is thus uniquely fitted to compose this history of the lineage of the Karmapas.

The biographies themselves have been compiled in the traditional manner from various Tibetan historical texts and the oral tradition. Subsequently their significance has been illuminated by Rinpoche's understanding of such sacred history. Throughout, the intention has been to reflect the pattern of spirituality revealed by the lives of the Karmapa, while also rendering an accurate historical outline of the lineage.

David Stott
Spiritual Representative
of Karma Thinley, Rinpoche
at dharma centres in the U.K.
Manchester, U.K.
October, 1978

1
Karmapa Dusum Khyenpa
(1110–1193)

DUSUM KHYENPA was born in the snow range of Tray Shu in Do Kham in the year of the Iron Tiger (1110 C.E.). From his parents, who were themselves accomplished practitioners, Dusum Khyenpa received instruction in *dharma.* At the age of eleven he had a vision of Mahākālī, the feminine energy aspect of the *dharmapāla,* thus manifesting his natural spirituality.

Five years later Dusum Khyenpa entered the monastic community as a novice, and subsequently studied the Yogācāra *mahāyāna* texts of the great philosopher Asaṅga from Geshe Jamarwa Chapa Cho Kyi Senge. During this period Dusum Khyenpa also studied Nāgārjuna and Candrakīrti's Madhyamaka texts from Lotsawa Patsap Nyima Drak. In addition he received the *tantric* teachings of the Kadampa lineage from Geshe Shawarapa.

At the age of twenty Dusum Khyenpa was ordained as a monk by the abbot, Mal Duldzin. He remained with the abbot to study the *vinaya*[1] texts. From the great Ga Lotsawa, Dusum Khyenpa received Kālacakra teachings and the "path and fruit" (Tib.: *lam.'bras*) teachings of the Indian *tantric* saint, Virūpa.[2]

Now thirty years old, Dusum Khyenpa traveled to Dak Lha Gampo to meet his teacher Gampopa, the holder of the Kagyupa lineage. When they met, Gampopa instructed him in the "graduated path" (Tib.: *lam.rim*) of the Kadampa tradition as preliminary practice. He told Dusum Khyenpa that he should practice it as he himself had done.[3] Following this basic training in the *sūtra* approach, Gampopa empowered Dusum Khyenpa to perform the spiritual practice of Hevajra. During this empowerment Dusum Khyenpa saw that Gampopa became the body of light of Hevajra.

A little later, Dusum Khyenpa went into a *śamatha* ("tranquillity") meditation retreat for nine months on the advice of his teacher. Throughout this period he never unfolded his hands long enough for the perspiration on them to dry. Gampopa recognized him as his most gifted student and instructed him in *vipaśyanā* ("insight") meditation. He practiced this for three years until his development of insight was comparable to the sun dispelling clouds. At this time Gampopa told him, "You have severed your bond with phenomenal existence. Now you will not return to *saṃsāra.*" He gave Dusum Khyenpa the oral instructions of *mahāmudrā* and teachings on the symbolic deity, Vajrayoginī. Gampopa told him to practice this at Kampo Gangra in Kham, and prophesied he would attain enlightenment at that place.

Dusum Khyenpa traveled first to Shau Tago, where he constructed a small retreat hut called Drub Zhi Densa ("square seat"), in which he practiced *mahāmudrā.* He attained the realization that *saṃsāra* and *nirvāṇa* are inseparably nondual (Tib.: *'khor.'das.yer.med*). Word reached him that his teacher had died, so he returned to Dak Lha Gampo monastery, where in a visionary experience he saw his teacher in the sky.

Dusum Khyenpa recalled his teacher's instructions for practice in the Kampo Gangra area. The mountain deity, Kampo Dorje Paltseg, symbolic embodiment of the area's elemental energy, invited him in a vision. Phagmo Drupa, another student of Gampopa, from whom came the eight minor lineages of the Dakpo Kagyu, entreated him not to go, saying, "If you go to Kham you will have to give many empowerments. This will shorten your life." Dusum Khyenpa said in reply, "Thank you for your kind advice, but regardless of what I do, I shall live until I am eighty-four."

At the age of fifty, he journeyed to Kampo Nenang where he immediately attained enlightenment through the practice of dream *yoga.* Dusum Khyenpa realized the essential sameness of day and night, dreams and the waking state, meditation and everyday life. His realization corresponded to the fourth level of *mahāmudrā,* which is known as "beyond meditation" (Tib.: *bsgom.med*).[4]

Spiritually, the moment of his enlightenment was symbolized in the visionary offering by *ḍākinīs* of a black *vajra* crown woven out of their hair. This crown is said to be symbolically present above the heads of all the Karmapa incarnations signifying their realization of the true nature of reality.

At this time, the nine deity *maṇḍala* of Hevajra and the fifteen deity *maṇḍala* of his wisdom consort, Nairātmyā, as well as many other *yidams* appeared in a vision to Dusum Khyenpa. Through his accomplishment of "dream *yoga*"[5] he "traveled" to Ceylon, where the *tantric* saint, Vajraghaṇṭā,[6] empowered him in the spiritual practice of the symbolic deity, Cakrasaṃvara, and to Tuṣita, the spiritual environment of the future Buddha, Maitreya, who instructed him in *bodhisattva* vows.

Dusum Khyenpa remained in Kampo Nenang for eighteen years, during which time he built a monastery and a retreat center. The fame of his spiritual realization spread and he became known as "the knower of the three times—past, present and future" (Tib.: *dus.gsum.mkhyen.pa*), indicating his transcending of time through his understanding of the unborn nature of mind.

The Kashmiri *paṇḍita,* Śākyaśrī,[7] who had been invited to Tibet to establish a new ordination lineage for the monastic community, declared Dusum Khyenpa was the "one of buddha-activity" or Karmapa, prophesied by Śākyamuni Buddha in the *Samādhirājasūtra.* Lama Zhang, founder of the Tsalpa Kagyu lineage confirmed this. The two teachers further said that Dusum Khyenpa embodied the principle of awakened compassion (Skt.: *avalokiteśvara*) and that following the age of Buddha Maitreya, the Karmapa Lama would be reborn as the Buddha Siṃha.

At the age of seventy-four Karmapa Dusum Khyenpa journeyed to the Drelong area of Kham, which was troubled by disputes. He pacified factional feuding and brought a time of peace. Moreover, he worked extensively for the sick, curing many diseases including blindness and paralysis. The healing power of his compassion was extremely potent. He also established monasteries at Mar Kham and Karma Gon, where he met Drogon Rechen, his principal student and holder of the lineage.

Toward the end of his life, Dusum Khyenpa returned to Dak Lha Gampo as he had been instructed to do by Gampopa. He made offerings to the monastery, repaired some of the buildings, and gave many teachings to the community there. Subsequently Karmapa established his principal monastic seat at Tsurphu, which remained the seat of the Karmapas until 1959. The abbot of Bodhgayā monastery in India sent a conch-shell horn to Tsurphu as a gift and as an acknowledgement of Dusum Khyenpa's powerful expression of *dharma.*

While he was at Tsurphu, Dusum Khyenpa brought to an end the disputes which Lama Zhang of the Tsala Kagyu lineage was engaged in. Lama Zhang was a great *siddha* and the ruler of the kingdom of Tsalpa, but had a rather aggressive nature which Karmapa alone was able to pacify.

One night while he was practicing dream *yoga,* Dusum Khyenpa received the spiritual practice of the four-faced twelve-armed Vajrayoginī from the *tantric* saint Indrabhūti.[8] Subsequently, during another visionary experience he received teachings from Vajrayoginī. Karmapa instructed his own students in these teachings, but a little while later he dreamt that five girls dressed in red and adorned with jewels appeared to him and said, "Do not give secret *vajrayāna* teachings to everybody who asks for them."

A few days later Dusum Khyenpa again gave the teachings and that very night the five girls appeared to him again in his dreams saying, "We are messengers of Princess Lakṣmīṅkarā.[9] Do not give secret *vajrayāna* teachings to everybody who asks for them." Three days later Karmapa gave the teachings to Lama Khampa Kungba, and that night in his dreams the girls appeared in the sky riding white clouds saying, "We told you not to give this secret *vajrayāna* teaching to everyone who asked for it, but you did not listen."

In the three months before Karmapa Dusum Khyenpa's death there were an unusually large number of rainbows, slight earth tremors and rumbling noises which people said were the drums of the *ḍākinīs.* The play of the elements seemed to be heralding some momentous event. At the age of eighty-four, on the first day of the year of the Water Ox (1194 C.E.) Dusum Khyenpa placed Tsurphu monastery, together with his books and relics, in the care of his principal student, Drogon Rechen. He also entrusted him with the letter in which he had predicted the circumstances into which the next Karmapa would be born. He distributed all his other possessions among the Kagyu communities.

In the morning of the third day of the new year, Dusum Khyenpa instructed his students in *dharma* for the last time. Then, sitting up, he gazed into the sky and entered into meditation. At noon he passed away.

During his death rites a week later many people had visionary experiences; some seeing his body in the smoke that rose from the funeral pyre, others seeing many suns in the sky and *ḍākas* and *ḍākinīs* dancing among them.

When the flames of the pyre died away, Dusum Khyenpa's heart, signifying his love, and his tongue, symbolizing his teaching, were found intact among the ashes. His students also recovered some of his bones, which appeared to have seed-syllables (Skt.: *bīja*) marked on them and other symbolic relics.

Karmapa's ashes were enshrined in a *stūpa* modeled after the one a Dhānyakaṭaka in southern India, where Śākyamuni Buddha had given the teachings of Kālacakra. This *stūpa* was desposited at Tsurphu monastery.

Dusum Khyenpa had many accomplished students through whom his influence penetrated into other traditions as well as his own Kaṃtshang Kagyu. The holder of his lineage was Drogon Rechen, who subsequently passed it to Pomdrakpa, who in turn gave it to the second Karmapa Lama. Four important founders of other lineages who received some teaching from Dusum Khyenpa were Taglung Thangpa, founder of the Taglung Kagyu; Lingje Repa, the great *mahāmudrā* practitioner and spiritual ancestor of the Drukpa Kagyu; Tsangpa Gyare, the actual founder of the Drukpa Kagyu; and Lama Kadampa Desheg, who founded the Katok Nyingma lineage. In addition, there were five students who had developed special powers. They were Dechung Sangjay in the area of telepathic ability, Dagden Batsa in the area of performing miracles, Tawa Kadampa in the area of special *bodhisattva* powers, Drogon Rechen in the area of blessing and Ge Chutsun in the area of profound realization.

2

Karmapa Karma Pakshi

(1206–1283)

THE SECOND KARMAPA, Karma Pakshi, was born in 1206 C.E. into a family descended from the eighth-century *dharma*-king, Trisong Detsun. His parents, who were devout religious practitioners, named their son Chodzin.

Chodzin was a precocious child and by the age of six he could read and write perfectly. By the time he was ten years old he had already grasped the essence of Buddhist doctrine. In addition to his intellectual ability, Chodzin also possessed an intuitive aptitude to rest the mind in stillness. As a result of this natural facility, when his meditation teacher, Pomdrakpa, introduced him to the nature of his own mind, he was able to develop spontaneous insight.

Pomdrakpa had himself received the teachings of the Karma Kagyu lineage from Drogon Rechen, the heir to Dusum Khyenpa's transmission. When he first bestowed an empowerment on Chodzin, he explained that in a vision he had seen Dusum Khyenpa and other teachers of the lineage surrounding his young student's residence, illustrating the latter's importance. In a further vision, Dusum Khyenpa revealed to Pomdrakpa that Chodzin was in fact his incarnation. From this time on, Pomdrakpa recognized Chodzin as the second Karmapa Lama and entitled him *dharma* master (Tib.: *chos.kyi.bla.ma*). In addition he ordained Karma Pakshi as a novice.

For eleven years Karma Pakshi studied with Pomdrakpa, specializing in the *mahāmudrā* teachings of Saraha and Gampopa. With his natural ability he was able to accomplish the teachings as quickly as he received them. At the conclusion of this period of study Pomdrakpa told him that he had developed his own understanding sufficiently but that he also needed to have a lineage of empowerments, textual transmissions and instructions from Śākyamuni or Vajradhara in order to teach others. He gave Karma Pakshi the complete series of Kagyu teachings, and thus became his spiritual father. When Karma Pakshi received the empowerment of Mahākāla he experienced the actual presence of the *dharmapāla*.

At the age of twenty-two Karma Pakshi was ordained a monk by Lama Jampa Bum, abbot of the Katok Nyingmapa monastery, established by Kadampa Desheg, the student of the first Karmapa. In his own spiritual practice at this time, Karma Pakshi concentrated upon "inner heat *yoga*" combined with *mahāmudrā* itself. In this way he developed both the form and formless aspects of *tantric* practice.

This was a period of civil disturbances in Kham and Karma Pakshi responded to the needs of the people by touring the area in an attempt to bring about peace. The whole area with its fields, mountains and valleys appeared to him as an environment of complete happiness (Tib.: *bde. mchog*) which contained the potential for the spread of *dharma*. This was symbolized in his vision of Mahāsukha Cakrasaṃvara surrounded by the dance of *ḍākas* and *ḍākinīs*. Later, inspired by the Vajra Black-Cloaked Mahākāla (Tib.: *rdo.rje.ber.nag.can*), who subsequently became the main *dharma* protector of the Karma Kagyu lineage, Karma Pakshi built a new monastery in the area of Sharchok Pungri in Kham.

In another vision, Karma Pakshi was instructed by a *ḍākinī* to develop communal singing of the six-syllable *mantra* of Avalokiteśvara, embodiment of enlightened compassion.[1] Karma Pakshi and his monks chanted the *mantra* as they traveled. From this time onward communal singing of the six-syllable *mantra* became an important part of popular religious practice in Tibet.

Karma Pakshi stayed at his new monastery for eleven years, engaged in intensive meditation practice. The fame of his spiritual power reached as far as Jang and China. Through his mastery of the energy of the four elements, Karma Pakshi pacified his environment. This was confirmed by the symbolic commitment of the mountain deity, Dorje Paltseg, to protect the Karma Kagyu lineage.

Subsequently, Karma Pakshi visited Karma Gon monastery, which had fallen into a state of disrepair. He restored it to its former condition. Then, inspired by Mahākālī, Karma Pakshi journeyed to Tsurphu and again carried out restoration work. Six years later, he went to the Tsang area of western Tibet via Lake Namtsho, where he obtained treasure which was used for the debts incurred during the restoration of the monastery.

In 1251 Karma Pakshi received an invitation from Prince Kublai who at that time ruled the Sino-Tibetan border regions. In response, Karma Pakshi traveled to the Wu-tok palace, reaching there in the year 1254, after being welcomed by a large army at Serta on the way.

Karma Pakshi was aware of the importance of his visit for the future of Kagyupa teachings and had many visionary experiences indicating this after his arrival at the court. He was honored by Kublai Khan, who requested him to display his spiritual power to the other religious teachers. Karma Pakshi complied with this request and also conducted himself with such courtesy that all acknowledged his greatness. The khan asked him to remain at his court permanently, but Karma Pakshi declined, forseeing the potential for trouble in the factional interests at the court.

At this time, the rest of China was under the control of Mongka Khan, a grandson of Genghis Khan, who had deposed his own cousin, Godin. Mongka Khan exercised a rather tenuous control of his younger brother Kublai. During this period the Sakyapa school had spread its teachings throughout China, due largely to the work of Sakya Paṇḍita (1182–1251) and his nephew, Phakpa (1235–1284).

Inspired by Avalokiteśvara and Mahākāla, Karma Pakshi decided to travel to northern Tibet. Despite Kublai Khan's anger at his refusal to stay, he journeyed to the Sino-Tibetan border region of Minyak. When he arrived the country was rocked by a tornado, which Karma Pakshi envisaged as the manifestation of the Vajra Black-Cloaked Mahākāla. He also had a vision of Vaiśravaṇa, protector of wealth, who requested him to remain in Minyak in order to construct a new temple there.

By 1256 Karma Pakshi had reached Amdo in northeastern Tibet, where he learned that Mongka Khan had suppressed the power of his younger brother, Kublai, and was now the supreme ruler of Mongolia and a large part of China. At this point, Mongka Khan invited him to return to China to teach *dharma*. The invitation was accepted and Karma Pakshi traveled slowly back to China, passing through the Minyak region once again. In a visionary experience, he was inspired by the red Tārā to go to Mongka Khan's palace in Liang Chou. By this time the far-ranging importance of Karma Pakshi's *dharma* activity had become very clear. On the journey to Mongka Khan's court he removed both environmental and social imbalances by his compassionate activity.

Karma Pakshi arrived at the court at the beginning of the winter. The khan marked his arrival by freeing prisoners in his honor and Karma

Pakshi manifested the enlightened compassion of Avalokiteśvara by giving many empowerments, textual transmissions and instructions. The khan became his devoted student and Karma Pakshi revealed that he had in fact studied with the first Karmapa, Dusum Khyenpa, in his previous life, and indeed had achieved the same *mahāmudrā* realization as Karma Pakshi himself.

In order to display the superb skillful means of the *dharma*, Karma Pakshi invited many jealous Taoist masters from Shen Shing, Tao Shi, and Er Kao to join him in debate. However, none were equal to it and they all accepted his teaching.

At the Alaka palace, Karma Pakshi empowered the khan and his other students in the spiritual practice of Cakrasaṃvara. Mongka Khan practiced his instruction so precisely that he was able to visualize the *yidam* in perfect detail. Later, through the power of Karma Pakshi's meditation, a vision of Saraha and the other eighty-four *tantric* saints appeared in the sky, where they remained for three days. The power of his teaching cut through the khan's involvement with politics, enabling him to develop an intuitive realization of *mahāmudrā*.

Karma Pakshi's influence extended far beyond the royal court and indeed had a profound effect on Sino-Mongol culture. He continued the process begun by Sakya Paṇḍita. As an example of this, Karma Pakshi advised that all Mongol Buddhists should avoid meat-eating on the days of the moon's phases. Similarly, non-Buddhists were advised to keep their own religious precepts on these days. The ten virtues[2] enunciated by Śākyamuni Buddha were emphasized as the basis of individual and social morality. Karma Pakshi's work for the welfare of the people was very extensive. For example, on thirteen separate occasions groups of prisoners were freed from confinement on his urging. Despite his own personal prestige, Karma Pakshi did not seek to advance the Karma Kagyu school at the expense of the other Buddhist traditions, but urged the khan to support them as well.

Subsequently the khan invited his guru to accompany him on a tour of his empire. At Karakorum, the Mongol's capital city, Karma Pakshi entered into a friendly dialogue with the representatives of other religious traditions. The party traveled on to the Sino-Mongolian border regions and then journeyed to Minyak. Here, inspired by the memory of Dusum Khyenpa, Karma Pakshi decided to return to Tibet. Mongka Khan had wanted his guru to accompany him to Manchuria, but Karma Pakshi declined, pointing to the impermanent nature of all situations. The khan did not attempt to detain him but granted him a safe conduct pass through all Mongol territories.

However, in the year of the Iron Tiger, as Karma Pakshi returned to Tibet, trouble broke out in China upon the death of Mongka Khan. At first Alapaga, the late khan's son, established his rule in spite of the fact that some Mongol chiefs supported the rival claim of his uncle, Kublai Khan. Soon, however, Kublai Khan was able to seize control and Alapaga was killed, reputedly by the magical power of a student of Lama Zhang of the Tsalpa Kagyu lineage.

At this time Karma Pakshi, whose journey had been delayed by local warfare, was inspired by a vision to construct a large statue of the Buddha, on his return to Tibet. However, he was acutely aware of the difficulties in the way of such a project. The way through these obstructions was revealed to him in a dream of a white horse which rescued him from danger. He composed a song to celebrate this in which he declared, "This supreme horse is like a golden bird. I, myself, am the supreme man, as was Siddhārtha Guatama. Therefore we will cross over these dangerous times."

Word reached Karma Pakshi that Kublai Khan, encouraged by court intrigue, had developed a grudge against him. The khan felt that he had been slighted by Karma Pakshi and that the latter had encouraged his rival and brother, Mongka Khan, so he decided to order his assassination.

The new khan's soldiers detained Karma Pakshi and subjected him to various indignities and tortures such as burning, poisoning and being thrown off a cliff, but in the face of this brutal treatment he manifested the compassion of Avalokiteśvara and the natural freedom of a *mahāsiddha*. Karma Pakshi's realization of the unborn and undying nature of mind meant that his captors were unable to harm him. Eventually he expressed great pity for their confusion.

These events forced Kublai Khan to reconsider his attitude to Karma Pakshi. Instead of assassination, exile seemed appropriate. The khan attempted to damage Karma Pakshi's health by sending him to a deserted area near the ocean where there were few people to receive the *dharma*. However, within the next few years Karma Pakshi spent his time composing texts and slowly recovered. Eventually Kublai Khan relented and apologized, asking Karma Pakshi to stay with him. When Karma Pakshi replied that he had to return to Tibet, the khan allowed him to depart saying, "Please remember me and pray for me and bless me. You are free to go and teach *dharma* wherever you wish."

Karma Pakshi arrived back at Tsurphu after a long journey and set to work constructing the statue of Buddha. The cast brass statue, named "Great Sage, Ornament of the World" (Tib.: *thub.chen dzam.gling.rgyan*), stood fifty-five feet tall and contained relics of the Buddha and his disciples. On completion the statue appeared to tilt to one side. Seeing this, Karma Pakshi entered into meditation, tilting his body in the same way. As he straigthened up, the statue righted itself.

Before his death in 1283, Karma Pakshi transmitted his lineage to his great student, Urgyenpa. He informed Urgyenpa that his next incarnation would come from western Tibet.

Karma Pakshi was both a profound *tantric* saint and scholar. The energy of his teachings inspired many people to travel the spiritual path. In addition to Urgyenpa, his other famous students included Maja Changchub Tsondru, Nyenre Gendun Bum and Mongka Khan.

3

Karmapa Rangjung Dorje

(1284–1339)

ON THE EIGHTH DAY of the first month of the year of the Wood Monkey (1284 C.E.) the third Karmapa incarnation, Rangjung Dorje, was born in the Tingri area of western Tibet. It is said that as his mother gave birth to him, the moon was rising and the baby immediately sat up saying, "The moon has risen."

The young Rangjung Dorje displayed extraordinary precocity. One day, at the age of three, while playing with friends, he suddenly asked them to make him a throne. When the imitation throne was constructed, he sat upon it, put on a black hat and announced that he was the Karmapa Lama.

Soon news of this remarkable child traveled far and wide, reaching the attention of Lama Urgyenpa. This Drukpa Kagyupa *lama* requested that the now five year old Rangjung Dorje be brought to see him. The spiritual qualities of the young child led Urgyenpa to realize that this was indeed the incarnation of the Karmapa. To renew the relationship between them, Lama Urgyenpa then bestowed the empowerments of Cakrasaṃvara and Hevajra upon Rangjung Dorje.

The education and training of the new Karmapa began at the age of seven, when he received the novice ordination from Lama Kunden Sherab. Following this he was formally enthroned as the Karmapa Lama at Tsurphu. His training continued at Tsurphu, where for eleven years he studied the complete teachings of the Kagyu and Nyingma traditions from Lama Nyenre Gendun Bum and Lama Namtshowa. The former saw Rangjung Dorje as an embodiment of Saraha, the great Indian *tantric* saint. He completed this intensive period of study with a meditation retreat in the vicinity of the great "Lady of the White Snows," Jomo Gangkar, known elsewhere as Mount Everest.

At the age of eighteen, Rangjung Dorje traveled to the great Kadampa monastery of Sangphu, where he received the full ordination from the abbot, Sakya Zhonnu. He remained for some time at the monastery, engaged in a wide study of philosophy, logic and religious law. His studies included the *vinaya,* thought transformation (Tib.: *blo.sbyong*), *The Five Texts of Maitreya* (Tib.: *'byams.chos.lde.lnga*)[1] Madhyamaka philosophy, *abhidharma,*[2] and the *Prajñāpāramitā sūtra* and *śāstra* commentaries.

The third Karmapa was an omnivorous student. Although he retained understanding from his previous lives, he researched all aspects of both contemporary and traditional learning. He received teachings from the most profound scholars of his day. As an example of this, some of the teachings he received from Lama Kunga Dondrup are particularly noteworthy, *viz:*

Kālacakra Tantra: root text and commentary
Guhyasamāja Tantra
Cakrasaṃvara Tantra: root text and commentary
Yamāntaka teachings.[3]
Vajramālā teachings
Hevajra Tantra and commentaries
Saṃpuṭika[4]
Guhyagarbha teachings
"The peaceful and wrathful deities" teaching[5]
Shi Jaypa teachings of Dampa Sangjay
Machig Labdron's *chod* teaching
Sakyapa path and fruit teachings
The *ṣaḍaṅga yoga* of Kālacakra[6]
Kanjur and *Tanjur* textual transmission[7]
A comparative study of Hindu philosophy

When Rangjung Dorje received the empowerment of Kālacakra, he had a visionary experience of the entire universe as contained within the body itself. Inspired by this, he composed a very influential text on astrology.

When this period of study with Lama Kunga Dondrup was completed, Rangjung Dorje entered into intensive meditation at the Garuḍa Castle retreat center near Tsurphu. During this retreat he had a dream in which the teachings of the philosopher Nāgārjuna were conveyed to him by his late guru, Urgyenpa.

Rangjung Dorje's studies extended into the medical field. From Lama Bare he received the *Sowa Rikpa* medical education. Subsequently, the

Karmapa stayed for a while with the learned Abbot Tsultim Rinchen, from whom he received teachings, among which are the following:

Guhyasāmaja Tantra
Madhyamaka philosophy
Mahāmāyā Tantra
Hevajra teachings, from the lineage of Ngok Chodor and Meton Tsonpo[8]
Yamāntaka Tantras
Cakrasaṃvara Tantras.

Later, Rangjung Dorje studied with Rigdzin Kumārarāja, the most important contemporary exponent of the innermost essence (Tib.: *snying. thig*) teachings of the Nyingmapa tradition. These teachings, which had been introduced into Tibet in the eighth century by the *paṇḍita,* Vimalamitra, reveal the direct experience of buddhahood through the nakedness of awareness. They had a lasting influence on Rangjung Dorje. In meditation he had a vision in which Vimalamitra was actually absorbed into his forehead. The effect of this teaching on Rangjung Dorje led to his bringing together the two teachings of Kagyupa "great seal" and Nyingmapa "great perfection" into one stream.

Rangjung Dorje's depth and breadth of scholarship was of a degree usually associated with the European "renaissance man," and in Tibet with the later Rime ("boundaryless") movement. Having assimilated most of the Buddhist teachings, empowerments and textual transmissions, which had been brought to Tibet, he communicated his vision in many important texts. Of the ones surviving, the foremost for the Kagyu sect is the *Deep Inner Meaning* (Tib.: *zab.mo.snang.don*), an invaluable commentary on the nature of *tantra.*

On the completion of his studies, Rangjung Dorje began to travel through southern Tibet, giving teachings and bestowing empowerments. He stayed in the Kongpo area for a period of three years. Many people were inspired to study *dharma* by the power of his presence and reputation as a *dharma* master.

In time, Rangjung Dorje's fame spread as far as the Mongol Emperor Togh Temur, who invited him to visit. He accepted the invitation and set out for China, but on the way his party was held up by unseasonable weather. The following spring the party again set out for China. On the way certain omens occurred which indicated to Rangjung Dorje that the emperor had died. Before continuing Karmapa performed the death rites for the emperor. The party finally arrived at the palace of Tai-ya Tu on the eighteenth day of the tenth month of the year of the Water Monkey (1332 C.E.). There it was learned that the Emperor Togh Temur had indeed died on the day of the omens. However, the royal family and court were still able to welcome Rangjung Dorje.

Karmapa advised the late emperor's younger brother, Toghon Temur, to wait for six months before ascending the throne and he predicted that Toghon Temur would prove to be a great monarch. On the fifteenth day of the first month of the Water Bird year the new emperor was enthroned by Rangjung Dorje in a grand ceremony.

In the year of the Wood Dog, Karmapa set out on the return journey to Tibet to procure, as a gift for the emperor, some long life nectar, *tse chu* (Tib.: *tse.chu*), left near Samye by Padmasambhava. On the way he established many monasteries dedicated to Kagyu *dharma*. Of especial importance is the temple that he established at Wu-tai Shan, the Five Peaks of Mañjuśrī mountain in China.

On his return to Tibet, Rangjung Dorje was involved in teaching and resolving political problems. Subsequently, Karmapa received an invitation from Toghon Temur to revisit China. So in the year of the Fire Rat, Karmapa set out once again for China. Throughout the long journey Rangjung Dorje continually taught *dharma*. Upon his arrival, the emperor welcomed him joyfully and received the gift of the *tse chu* from Karmapa which enabled him to live the longest of the Mongol emperors. During his stay Rangjung Dorje established a new Kagyupa monastery. He was also able to end the climatic difficulties which were harming the crops in China at that time.

On the fourteenth day of the sixth month of the year of the Earth Rabbit (1339 C.E.), Rangjung Dorje told the emperor of his presentiments of his own imminent death. He withdrew into the Cakrasaṃvara shrine, where he meditated on the *heruka* and passed away in meditation. The next day, as his final teaching to the emperor and empress, Karmapa appeared to manifest his face in the full moon.

Rangjung Dorje's influence on *vajrayāna* Buddhism was incalculable. As well as his invaluable texts, his teaching was spread through his many accomplished students. Rangjung Dorje taught the famous Sakya scholar, Yagde Paṇḍita,[9] and also the most profound Nyingmapa guru, Longchen Rabjampa. In addition, Rangjung Dorje's other students included Shamar Rinpoche, Drakpa Senge and Toghon Temur.

4

Karmapa Rolpe Dorje

(1340–1383)

DURING THE PREGNANCY of Rolpe Dorje's mother many auspicious symbols occurred in her dreams, indicating the birth of an incarnate guru. On the eighth day of the third month of the year of the Iron Dragon (1340 C.E.) Karmapa Rolpe Dorje was born. The sounds of the six-syllable *mantra* were heard on the lips of the baby and a beautiful fragrance issued from the body.

As a young child Rolpe Dorje frequently displayed his remarkable abilities. At the age of three he declared "I am Karma Pakshi. Many of my students are here and so I have come." He spontaneously sat in the position of Amitābha and told his mother that the position was one in which he had been seated in her womb.

At the age of six the young prodigy, on being questioned about his previous lives, replied, "I am Dusum Khyenpa and Karma Pakshi. I went to China and began to pacify the Mongol armies. I am the one who watched from the clouds. My guru is emptiness and I myself am your guru. Now I possess three emanations. One is with the bodhisattva Ratnamati. One dwells in the spiritual environment of Buddha Akṣobhya and I am the third. At the moment you may doubt me but soon this will pass. You yourself are my student."

Subsequently Gon Gyalwa, who acted as one of Rolpe Dorje's tutors, questioned the boy about his incarnation as Rangjung Dorje, saying, "Karmapa said he would live to be the age of eighty-four but he died at fifty-five. What happened?" Rolpe Dorje replied, "Fewer people were religious and their way of life was very negative. This upset Rangjung Dorje and caused him to lose his wish to remain here." Gon Gyalwa further questioned the young incarnation about why people had seen his face in the full moon on the night following his death. The young boy answered by saying, "Rangjung Dorje had limitless compassion and his students had strong devotion. These two causes coincided and produced the vision of his appearance in the moon."

The young Rolpe Dorje had many spontaneous visionary experiences, which symbolized the natural unfoldment of his own spirituality. At one time when he fell ill with influenza, he entered into meditation upon Bhaiṣajyaguru the buddha-embodiment of medicine. In this meditation he drank from the crystal water bowl which Bhaiṣajyaguru extended to him. Immediately his sickness passed. Rolpe Dorje experienced the omnipresence of the buddha-nature throughout being. It is said that he was able to see the different buddha "families"[1] in his own veins and to see the spiritual environments of buddhas in one atom. On one occasion he manifested ten different forms in which he listened to ten different teachings in ten different spiritual environments. These experiences reflected Rolpe Dorje's realization of the interpretation of buddha-nature in all experience and phenomena.

The awakening of the young Karmapa's innate compassion was symbolized by his visionary descent to hell in the form of Avalokiteśvara. There he controlled the sufferings brought about by intense aggression. With the rain of his compassion he was able to extinguish the fires of hatred and restore all the beings trapped in their environment to basic sanity.

The Karmapa child was like a *garuḍa,* the mythical bird which hatches from the egg complete full-grown. In his dreams he visited Uḍḍiyāṇa, land of the *ḍākinīs,* where Vajrayoginī gave him profound teachings in which she told him, "Yours is a naturally unborn mind. Let meditation, visualization and recitation arise. Make offering prayers and *tormas.* By performing this practice for eight days, you will obtain the spiritual power of Vajrayoginī."

In other dreams Rolpe Dorje journeyed to the Potala spiritual environment. Here he perceived the *maṇḍala* of Avalokiteśvara in its pure immediacy, which produced in him the realization of *mahāmudrā.*

To express his understanding, Rolpe Dorje composed songs relating his visionary experiences. At the age of nine he began to study the teachings of the Kagyu and Nyingma traditions. During this period it is said that Rolpe Dorje accomplished his studies with great ease, apparently having to exert very little effort, due to his inherent ability.

When Rolpe Dorje reached the age of thirteen he went to central Tibet. On the way he passed Dak Lha Gampo, the monastery of Gampopa, which he saw as a *stūpa* made of jewels, surrounded by buddhas, *bod-*

hisattvas and saints. He composed a song in praise of the place to express his delight.

At Phagmo Dru monastery Rolpe Dorje was welcomed by Taisitu Changchub Gyaltsen, who became ruler of Tibet. From there he continued to Tsurphu, the principal monastery of the Karmapa Lamas. On his arrival he was inspired by a vision of Vajrayoginī. In preparation for his monastic ordination Rolpe Dorje studied the *vinaya* texts, concerning religious discipline. Then, at the age of fourteen he received ordination as a novice from Dondrup Pal Rinpoche. He was named Dharmakīrti to confirm his entrance into the monastic life.

Dondrup Pal Rinpoche evoked in Karmapa a sense of the richness of Dusum Khyenpa's transmission. In meditation he saw as many Dusum Khyenpas as stars in the sky. Following this, Rolpe Dorje's spiritual practice concerned Amitābha, the embodiment of deathlessness. He entered into a retreat in which the significance of Amitābha teachings became completely clear to him, both through his meditation and his dreams.

Subsequently Rolpe Dorje invited the Nyingmapa scholar Gyalwa Yongtonpa to visit him. This teacher was the living lineage-holder of the Karma Kagyu "transmission," which he himself had received from Rangjung Dorje. On meeting Yongtonpa, a spontaneous understanding of the *maṇḍala* of peaceful and wrathful deities arose in Rolpe Dorje. The old scholar said, "I am very old but Rangjung Dorje showed such kindness in teaching me that I have come from afar. Now please tell me what you remember of your previous lives."

Karmapa Rolpe Dorje replied that he was not able to recall his life as Dusum Khyenpa very clearly and that he could only remember a little of his life as Rangjung Dorje. However, he emphasized that he recalled his life as Karma Pakshi perfectly. When he heard this, Yongtonpa was overcome with emotion and prostrated at his young student's feet.

Rolpe Dorje received an exhaustive range of teachings, especially Kagyu and Nyingma instructions from Lama Yongtonpa. At the age of eighteen he was ordained a monk by the Abbot Dondrup Pal Rinpoche. During the same year Rolpe Dorje met the famous Sakya *lama,* Sonam Gyaltsen, from whom he received the empowerment of the red Avalokiteśvara. Each *lama* recognized the other's spiritual authority on their meeting.

The following year the Mongol Emperor Toghon Temur, who was anxious to restore his links with the Karmapa incarnations, invited Rolpe

Dorje to his court. However, at that time Karmapa was engaged in a teaching tour of Tibet and was unable to go. When he returned to Tsurphu a second invitation arrived from Toghon Temur in which the emperor said,

> I am the emperor, the king of heaven. I have heard that you, Karmapa Rolpe Dorje have been reborn for us and you now dwell in Tsurphu. Therefore, with deep respect I ask you to remember your previous actions. These are degenerate times, full of many sufferings. Consider these sufferings and also the innate goodness of the people. Please bestow on us the nectar of the *dharma* to make us joyful. Now many beings are acting in the wrong way, so please point to the right direction for them. Please set forth from home. Do not consider the difficulties of the journey nor your health but please come quickly. Buddha himself did not think of his own sufferings when he wished to benefit sentient beings. Please come immediately. When you arrive we must both encourage the progress of *buddhadharma* and the welfare of the people. Please listen, great Lama Rolpe Dorje.
>
> As an offering I am sending you shrine implements, one ingot of gold, three ingots of silver and eighteen rolls of silk brocade.
>
> Sent from Tai-ya Tu, the residence of the emperor, on the tenth day of the tenth month in the year of the Earth Monkey.

Karmapa began the long and difficult journey to Peking in the ninth month of the Earth Dog year, at the age of nineteen. He used much of his time on the journey in composing texts. When the party arrived in Shawo, the Mongol envoys suggested that fresh horses, yaks and bearers be requisitioned from the local populace. However, Rolpe Dorje said, "Please do not ask the people for anything. I shall send and provide for all. One should never burden the people." Despite this, people responded to Karmapa's compassionate concern and many offerings were made to him. Rolpe Dorje instructed the people in nonviolence and the development of a loving attitude. To those who were already engaged in meditation practice Rolpe Dorje gave the explanations of *mahāmudrā* and the six doctrines. At this time Rolpe Dorje himself attained the realization of *ati yoga,* the most sublime of Nyingma teachings.

Rolpe Dorje's journey lay through the area of Wu-t'ai Shan where he made a pilgrimage to the peaks of Mañjuśrī. There he met five Indian *yogins* who presented him with a *buddharūpa* carved by Nāgārjuna. During this period Rolpe Dorje composed a series of songs dedicated to Mañjuśrī.

Continuing with the journey, Karmapa was invited to visit the domain of Prince Saṅgha Śrī. He held a short seminary there during which he instructed both courtiers and members of the public. Rolpe Dorje was also able to help the local people by ending an invasion of locusts, which threatened to destroy the crops. As he passed through various tiny kingdoms he pacified factional feuding and witnessed the signing of many treaties. He donated a great deal of his wealth to restore peace and construct monasteries. In his *dharma* activity at this time Rolpe Dorje was inspired by Yamāntaka, who embodies the indestructibility of buddhahood. Yamāntaka removed the obstructing hindrances to Karmapa's compassionate work. Subsequently, Rolpe Dorje subdued the embodiments of the area's energy and in this way turned the area to Kagyu *dharma*.

Another notable event from the journey was Rolpe Dorje's visit to the famous "magical" temple of Sakya Paṇḍita. In Minyak Karmapa spread the *dharma* and also arranged a pardon for a ruler who had rebelled against the khan. His presence instilled in the people a reverence for the nonviolent way of life.

Finally on the eighteenth day of the twelfth month of the year of the Iron Mouse, the party arrived at the palace of Tai-ya Tu, where Rolpe Dorje was feted by the emperor and empress. Happily enough the empress gave birth to a baby, a son Maitrīpāla, later the same month. The commitment of the emperor to Kagyu *dharma* was evident and sincere and so Karmapa was able to instruct him in the vital triad of Kagyu teachings, namely Vajrayoginī, the six doctrines of Nāropa, and the *mahāmudrā* of Tilopa. Rolpe Dorje also gave the royal children a grounding in the basic precepts of Buddha and generally instructed the Chinese and Mongol peoples and the other ethnic minorities of the empire in the religion and nonviolence. As a present to his guru the emperor freed all prisoners and excused his monks from court etiquette. During his stay in China the compassionate activity of Rolpe Dorje extended to curing the sick and combating harsh climatic conditions.

After three years work in China, it was revealed in a dream to Rolpe Dorje that the emperor's life would be short. This made him decide to return to Tibet. Toghon Temur was upset by this news and pleaded with his guru to stay, saying, "Before you came everything was costly. Now things are easily obtained. Please remain here so that we may spread *dharma* in the manner of Kublai Khan and Sakya Phakpa. Please think carefully. All the factions who opposed the emperor are now peaceful. I have a new son. You are a fortunate teacher."

Rolpe Dorje replied, "I myself do not possess enough knowledge. It is better to cease pretending. What I can do is to bless emperors by invoking the principle of the three jewels and by teaching them. All my words have been written down. Now I must return to Tibet. Monks must go wherever they can benefit sentient beings. It is best not to be attached to any country." So, reluctantly the emperor let Rolpe Dorje go.

Karmapa departed in the first month of the Wood Tiger year. Again his journey was spent working for the welfare of the inhabitants of the various areas through which he passed. Together with the Sakya *lama,* Lhachen Sonam Solo, he saved the lives of condemned prisoners. Then he traveled through Minyak where he built a new monastery at Kora and spread the *dharma.*

Rolpe Dorje's timetable on the journey revolved around meditation, teaching and welfare work. All the gifts that he himself received he gave to needy individuals or institutions. When the party reached the Kongjo area in northeastern Tibet, it came across a smallpox epidemic. On the night following Karmapa's arrival, people said that they could hear noises on the roof of his house. In the morning Rolpe Dorje said that he had brought the epidemic to an end by manifesting as a *garuḍa* to destroy the imbalances producing the smallpox. Karmapa expressed his surprise at people's claims to have heard the noises of the *garuḍa,* because he said in actuality it was simply the activity of formless mind.

Rolpe Dorje had long been interested in Indian poetics. In Kongjo he had a dream in which Sarasvatī, symbolic consort of Mañjuśrī and embodiment of artistic energy, appeared to him. Sarasvatī gave him a pot of yoghurt and told him to drink it. The morning following this dream Rolpe Dorje discovered he had a new-found ability to understand poetics.

Arriving in the Tsongkha area near Lake Kokonor, Karmapa's party was honored by the local rulers. Rolpe Dorje gave teachings and distributed aid to the local inhabitants. At Lake Kokonor he composed his text, *Removing Erroneous Views* (Tib.: *lta.ba.nying.bsal*). It was in this area that Rolpe Dorje met a young boy who was destined to have a profound effect on Buddhism, Tsongkhapa. He gave the boy lay ordination and the name Kunga Nyingpo. Karmapa predicted about the child that, "This is a holy child who will be of great benefit to people. Therefore, he is like a second Buddha come to Tibet."

At this time Princess Punyadhari of Minyak, one of Rolpe Dorje's students, dreamt of a huge *thangka* of Śākyamuni Buddha, measuring eleven arm-spans from ear to ear. On hearing of this Karmapa devised a method to realize her dream. He rode over a certain area of ground on horseback tracing the pattern of this image with his horse's hoofprints. The measurements of Buddha's figure traced in this manner were found to be perfect. Then the image was transferred to a huge piece of silk. In all it took five hundred people thirteen months to complete the *thangka,* which also represented Mañjuśrī and Maitreya on either side of Śākyamuni. On completion the *thangka* was blessed by Rolpe Dorje. During the ceremony auspicious events occurred. Afterwards Princess Punyadhari gave the *thangka* to her guru. Later the princess requested Karmapa's counsel when her region was about to be invaded by a Mongol army. Rolpe Dorje, who had the perfect courage of nonviolence, invoked the principle of wisdom and compassion and the invading army moved away from the region. The people were overjoyed. Rolpe Dorje stayed for three months during which time the atmosphere was pervaded by love and kindness among mankind and all other creatures.

Karmapa's extensive activity in both *dharma* and social welfare attracted jealousy from certain quarters. Conspiracies were plotted to harm Rolpe Dorje, but nothing significant ever came of them. Karmapa himself followed as strict a regimen in the camp (Tib.: *gar.chen*) as in a settled monastery. From the time he awoke until nine in the morning, he performed his spiritual practices. From then until noon he gave instructions in *dharma.* At noon he performed prostrations and walking meditation. Throughout the afternoon he practiced Avalokiteśvara meditation, and in the evening he studied or composed texts. His nights were passed in the practice of dream *yoga.* Rolpe Dorje was, in fact, a vegetarian and established this as the basic diet of his camp.

Although surrounded by intrigue and gossip he remained unaffected and impartial. In contrast to many religious luminaries, Rolpe Dorje did not display great pleasure to financial sponsors, reserving this instead for good meditators. Wherever he went he worked assiduously for the welfare of others in any way possible, from building bridges to instruction in metaphysics. His career exemplified the qualities of a true *bodhisattva* and master of all facets of Buddha's teaching.

When Karmapa's party arrived in the Nangchen principality, his indisposition caused much concern. However, he informed people that it was not yet time for him to die. He further said that he would die in a very open land with many deer and wild horses. "If I become ill in such a country I will die," Rolpe Dorje declared. "So, do not lose any of my books." Then the party traveled to Karma Gon monastery, where he gave teaching to the monks.

Karmapa asked his students to bring some juniper wood on the next stages of the journey. He told them that it was the custom in China to use sandalwood or agaru on a funeral pyre for a respected person, but since Tibet did not have this kind of wood, they would have to use juniper wood. When the party reached Nakchu, one of the monks broke his hand. This was considered very inauspicious.

During this period Rolpe Dorje spoke to his students and attendants about the viciousness of *saṃsāra* and the widespread inability of people to follow *dharma.* He said, "Perhaps it is better to demonstrate the real nature of *saṃsāra,* which is that everything is impermanent." One of his students, Rekarwa, realized that Karmapa was referring to his own imminent demise and pleaded with him not to pass away. However, everybody else in the camp laughed at Rekarwa.

Subsequently the Karmapa's party set up camp in the barren northern plains of Tibet. Inauspicious signs were observed in the camp and Karmapa himself made oblique comments upon them. On the night of the full moon in the seventh month of the year of the Female Water Pig (1383 C.E.), Rolpe Dorje became sick. He gazed into space and recited the "Prayer of Samantabhadra." [2] Then he meditated until just before sunrise, when he passed away. The moments of his passing were marked by strange atmospheric occurrences, which symbolized to people the *ḍākas* and *ḍākinīs* greeting Rolpe Dorje. Many people throughout Tibet, who had personal connections with him, envisaged him in various personal manifestations at this time.

Rolpe Dorje's ashes were brought to Tsurphu monastery and enshrined as relics.

Among Karmapa Rolpe Dorje's principal students were Shamar Kachod Wangpo, Drigung Chokyi Drakpa and Lobzang Drakpa Tsongkhapa.

5
Karmapa Dezhin Shegpa
(1384–1415)

DEZHIN SHEGPA was born at sunrise on the eighteenth day of the sixth month of the year of the Wood Mouse (1384 C.E.) to the *yogin* Guru Rinchen and his wife, Lhamo Kyi. His mother's pregnancy had been rich in auspicious events and immediately after his birth, Dezhin Shegpa was heard to exclaim, "I bow down to all the buddhas. I am Karma Pakshi. *Oṃ maṇi padme hūṃ.*"

When he reached the age of five, Dezhin Shegpa was invited to Kongpo Ngakphu, where a great meditator called Shao had slipped on the ice and broken three of his ribs. The young incarnation massaged his ribs and Shao's injuries healed, causing him no further pain.

During this period Dezhin Shegpa received several empowerments and textual transmissions for later practice. These included the six doctrines of Nāropa and the *mahāmudrā* of Tilopa, the principal Kagyu instructions. At the age of seven he received novice ordination from the great abbot, Ngakphu Sonam Zangpo, with whom he went on to study the full range of *hīnayāna* and *mahāyāna* teachings. Then he was formally enthroned at Tsurphu monastery. He continued his education there with his tutor, until being ordained a monk at the age of nineteen in the largest ordination ceremony (eighty monks) ever held in Tibet.

Once his basic education was completed, Dezhin Shegpa began to tour. On his travels he met the Nyingma *terton* ("finder of hidden texts"), Sangye Lingpa, whom he had known in his previous incarnation. The *terton* presented him with a scarf and some gold, and Karmapa reminded him that he still possessed the previous Karmapa's walking stick. Sangye Lingpa was astonished by the power of Dezhin Shegpa's awareness and became very devoted to him. Traveling on, Karmapa received the empowerment of Vajramālā and other teachings from the saintly meditator, Yeshe Pal.

Subsequently, Dezhin Shegpa was invited to visit Kham. During this tour he was engaged in giving many teachings to both religious and lay people. The instructions he gave varied to suit his audience, covering all aspects of *dharma,* from basic *mahāyāna* precepts to the *tantric yoga* of the six doctrines. At the conclusion of the visit, Dezhin Shegpa returned to Tsurphu.

The fifth Karmapa concerned himself greatly with the reconciliation of divided communities and attempted to establish nonviolence as the norm of social and political behavior. He created protected reserves for wild animals, and also put an end to toll roads. Thus, his compassion expressed itself in both the social and religious spheres.

An important aspect of Dezhin Shegpa's career was his relationship with the Ming Emperor Yung Lo. The latter, inspired by a dream of Avalokiteśvara and also at the prompting of his wife, invited Karmapa to visit China in 1406 C.E. The letter of invitation read, "My father and both parents of the queen are now dead. You are my only hope, essence of buddhahood. Please come quickly. I am sending as offering a large ingot of silver, one hundred fifty silver coins, twenty rolls of silk, a block of sandalwood, one hundred fifty bricks of tea and ten pounds of incense."

On Dezhin Shegpa's arrival in Nanking three years later, he was welcomed by ten thousand monks. At the palace the emperor greeted him with a scarf and a precious shell, the spiral of which turned to the right. The emperor thought that if Karmapa really did have telepathic powers as people claimed, he would know his own wish that he should be given the same gifts in return. As the emperor was thinking this, Dezhin Shegpa pulled a scarf and a conch shell, spiralling to the right, out of his pocket and gave them to Yung Lo.

The emperor feted his new-found *guru,* giving him the place of honor on his left. As an indication of his devotion he gave Dezhin Shegpa a higher throne than his own. The reception room was full of offerings and food and entertainment were presented in abundance. Throughout the next month, while Karmapa rested after his long journey, the emperor and his court continued to shower him with presents. In this manner an atmosphere of surrender and devotion to the teachings was developed.

Finally, on the fifth day of the second month of the year of the Earth Mouse, Dezhin Shegpa began to teach. For the next two weeks he bestowed on the emperor and empress the empowerments of the red Avalokiteśvara, Vajrakīlaya, Guhyasamāja, Maitreya, Vajradhātu, Hevajra, Tārā, Vairocana, Bhaiṣajyaguru and the thousand-armed Avalokiteśvara. During these weeks Dezhin Shegpa revealed the miraculous nature of enlightened energy, awakened by the accomplishment of these *vajrayāna* teachings.

On the first day as the emperor made offerings of robes to his guru and the monks, a magical temple seemed to be present in space.

On the second day a rainbow reminiscent of a begging bowl appeared, followed by cloud formations resembling groups of *arhats.*[1]

On the third day the atmosphere was filled with fragrance and a sweet and gentle rain fell.

On the fourth day a brightly colored rainbow appeared over Dezhin Shegpa's house.

On the fifth day space appeared to be full of auspicious symbols and people were convinced that they could see *arhats* in the city streets.

On the sixth day many lights seemed to issue from Dezhin Shegpa's shrine.

On the seventh day an unearthly red glow came from the *buddharūpa* on the main temple and illuminated the grounds.

On the eighth day two lights appeared in space: one hovered over the royal burial ground and one hung over the emperor's palace.

On the ninth day a crowd of people claimed that they had observed an old monk who flew through the air and then disappeared at the door of the temple.

On the tenth day a crane and a bird like a blue *garuḍa* flew together in the sky.

On the eleventh day luminous rays seemed to stream to the east from Karmapa's temple and the house in which he was staying.

On the twelfth day there was a rain of flowers onto the emperor's palace.

On the thirteenth day people swore that they had seen several monks in the sky, who were saying prayers and making prostrations in the direction of Karmapa's residence.

On the fourteenth day the ceremonies were completed. A flock of cranes danced in the sky and clouds appeared in the shape of symbolic deities, *garuḍas,*[2] lions, elephants, *stūpas*[3] and dragons.

On the next day the Karmapa was honored by the emperor, who gave him an honorific Chinese name. On the following day a reception was given for Dezhin Shegpa in the royal palace. To complete the honor a final feast was held in Karmapa's residence. During these celebrations the display of *vajrayāna* energy invoked by Dezhin Shegpa continued.

Emperor Yung Lo decided that the apparently miraculous events which he had witnessed due to his devotion, should be recorded for posterity. He commissioned talented artists to represent them in painting on large rolls of silk, one of which was kept at Tsurphu. The emperor himself composed a literary account of the miracles, which was transcribed onto the paintings in five languages: Tibetan, Chinese, Mongol, Yugor and Turkic.

After the conclusion of the ceremonies and teachings, Dezhin Shegpa set out on a pilgrimage to Wu-tai Shan, the Five Peaks of Mañjuśrī. However, despite this separation from his guru, the emperor continued to experience the direct inspiration of his teaching as a result of his unshakeable devotion.

When Dezhin Shegpa returned from his pilgrimage he discovered that the emperor was busy with plans for an invasion of Tibet. Yung Lo attempted to rationalize his plans to his *guru,* saying, "I only want to send a small cavalry army to Tibet, because there are many different sects who might fight among themselves in the future. It would be better if they were all part of your sect. Then every year there could be a Tibetan religious council meeting in a different part of Tibet."

Karmapa was not seduced by the emperor's ambitious project and discouraged him by saying, "One sect cannot bring order to the lives of all types of people. It is not beneficial to think of converting all sects into one. Each individual sect is especially constituted so as to accomplish a particular aspect of good activity. So please do not send your army." Yung Lo was convinced by these words and acquiesced to his *guru*'s wishes.

In fact Dezhin Shegpa had subsequently to dissuade the emperor a second time from an invasion. This occurred when a Chinese ambassadorial mission in Tibet was attacked and destroyed by bandits near the Drigung monastery. When the emperor was informed of this, he prepared a punitive expedition but Karmapa was again able to convince him not to respond with counter-terror. In this manner Karmapa devoted himself to spreading the way of nonviolence and tolerance.

The emperor's relationship with Karmapa was one of deep sincerity and confidence. As a result of his devotion one day during a ceremony, Yung Lo perceived the boundless nature of Karmapa's spirituality, symbolized by the black *vajra* crown. The emperor realized that it was due to his own devotion to the *guru* that he had been able to see the black *vajra* crown, which is symbolically present above the heads of all the Karmapa incarnations. So he decided to have a replica made, ornamented with precious jewels and gold, which he gave to his *guru.* Dezhin Shegpa developed the ceremony in which he displayed this replica to people, while embodying the compassion of Avalokiteśvara. In this way he communicated the inspiration of his own spirituality. From this time on, the ceremony of the black *vajra* crown has become an integral feature of the *dharma* activity of the Karmapas.

In 1408 C.E., Dezhin Shegpa informed the emperor of his decision to return to Tibet. Yung Lo, who was upset by the news, said, "You are very kind to have come here but your stay has not been long. In former times an emperor was more powerful than his *guru,* but you, my *guru,* are more powerful than I am. I cannot prevent you from leaving now that you wish to go, but you must return when I request."

After a long journey, Dezhin Shegpa finally reached Tsurphu. He discovered that the monastery had been damaged by an earthquake and so he carried out repair work. In addition he directed the transcription of the *Tripiṭaka* in silver and gold. He then distributed wealth and food among the monks and people of central Tibet.

Karmapa was highly venerated by his contemporaries. Je Tsongkhapa sent a letter to Dezhin Shegpa in which he wrote, "You are like a second Buddha. I would like to see you but I am in a three year retreat. So I am sending you a statue of Maitreya which belonged to Atīśa."

Despite the enormous responsibility of guiding the Karma Kagyu school, Dezhin Shegpa never wavered from his attitude of gentleness and love. Trung Mase Togden, the founder of the Surmang complex of monasteries, once asked Karmapa to reprove his Karma Garchen people who had broken their commitments. Dezhin Shegpa told him, "In my whole life I have never been angry. I could never be angry." One story about Dezhin Shegpa tells of a lazy student who preferred sleep to meditation. However, during his sleep the smiling countenance and sometimes the whole upper body of Dezhin Shegpa would appear to him. Shocks like this instilled a new sense of urgency in the lazy student and he became an assiduous meditator.

In 1415 Dezhin Shegpa was invited to visit Kham, but he declined saying that he would meet the Khampa people soon in any case. Later that year Karmapa contracted small pox, which proved fatal. Having instructed his monks to guard his books and his religious artifacts, he passed away on the day of the full moon, in his thirty-first year. After his body was cremated, many different images of deities such as Guhyasamāja and Hevajra appeared on his bones.

The principal students of the fifth Karmapa were Trung Mase Togden, Emperor Yung Lo and Shamar Chophel Yeshe, as well as the Drigung Kagyu, Chen-Nga Dondrup Gyalpo and Minyak Tokden.

6

Karmapa Thongwa Donden

(1416–1453)

IN 1416 C.E. the sixth Karmapa incarnation, Thongwa Donden, was born in Ngom near Karma Gon monastery in Kham. Thus the prediction of the previous Karmapa to the Khampa people was fulfilled. His parents were both faithfully religious. During the mother's pregnancy they had had significant dreams and at birth recognized their baby to be a very exceptional child.

When he was only a few months old, Thongwa Donden was taken by his parents to Lama Ngompa Jadral, a student of the fifth Karmapa. The young child was very affected by this meeting and began to recite the alphabet. Ngompa Jadral then asked the infant his true identity. In reply Thongwa Donden said, "I am the unborn, free from all names, places, and I am the glory of all that lives. I shall lead many to liberation."

Subsequently, the third Shamar Rinpoche, Chopel Yeshe, officially recognized him as the sixth Karmapa Lama and ceremonially enthroned him. During his infancy Karmapa Thongwa Donden was taken on a tour of Kagyupa monasteries, where his precocious qualities made a vivid impression on people. He met with the first Trungpa *tulku,* Kunga Gyaltsen, at Surmang monastery and astounded him by asking, "Where is the protection cord I gave you in my last incarnation?" Lama Trungpa was overcome with emotion as he produced the cord and bowed down to his *guru.*

The young Thongwa Donden rediscovered his own natural spirituality through visionary experiences of many symbolic deities. In 1424, at the age of eight, Thongwa Donden was ordained as a novice by the abbot Sonam Zangpo, and received the *bodhisattva* vows. He began to receive instruction in the actual texts and practices of *dharma* from the great saint Ratnabhadra, who was an incarnation of Rechungpa. From this *lama* the young Karmapa received the empowerments and textual transmissions of

Vajrayoginī, Hevajra and the *mahāmudrā*. Shamar Rinpoche communicated the doctrines of Tilopa to him in addition to other Karma Kagyu teachings.

Thongwa Donden's religious education was not confined to the Kaṃtshang tradition, but also included the five *tantras* and six doctrines of Niguma,[1] both deriving from the Shangpa Kagyu, and also the *Duk Ngal Shijay*[2] doctrine of the Indian preceptor Phadampa Sangye.

During his teenage years the sixth Karmapa concentrated heavily on developing a consistent Kaṃtshang liturgical system. Since the primary emphasis of the Karma Kagyu had been on meditation itself, hence its alternate styling as the "Meditative Tradition" (Tib.: *sgrub.brgyud*), liturgy and ritual had tended to be neglected. What liturgy was employed by Karma Kagyupas was largely borrowed from other traditions. Thongwa Donden sought to establish a firm basis for a specifically Kaṃtshang liturgy, and wrote many Kaṃtshang sādhana rituals.

He composed spiritual practices of the two highly important Kagyu *yidams,* Vajrayoginī and Cakrasaṃvara, and also wrote a long version of the *Preliminary Practices* (Tib.: *sngon.'gro*). Thongwa Donden evolved a new style of recitation and chanting. In addition he composed a large treatise on Mahākāla dance and liturgy. The sixth Karmapa's visionary qualities added a special power and depth to his endeavors in this field.

At the completion of this period of literary activity, Karmapa received the full ordination and then set out on a tour of central Tibetan monasteries. On this journey Thongwa Donden was inspired by many visionary experiences. In one vision he saw Mahākāla together with his wisdom consort and received from them special teachings on the six *yogas* of Nāropa and the *mahāmudrā* of Tilopa. At another place he envisaged Tilopa, Milarepa and Vimalamitra in a vision which thus united the streams of *mahāmudrā* and *mahā ati.* Later Vajradhara, accompanied by the first Karmapa, Dusum Khyenpa, appeared to him, symbolizing the power of the Kagyu tradition. In another vision, Thongwa Donden saw the Indian *tantric* saint Ḍombhi Heruka.[3] and his consort, riding on a tiger. Ḍombhi Heruka revealed to him that he was perfectly pure and free of all obscurations.

In Lhasa the sixth Karmapa met the famous Sakya abbot, Kunchen Rongtonpa,[4] who bestowed upon him a great number of doctrines. Rongtonpa was delighted by Thongwa Donden's brilliance and declared, "I have Buddha as my student." Around this time Karmapa repaired the damage and decay at Sangphu and Ngakphu monasteries. Then he traveled to Tsurphu and thence to Kham. Due to Thongwa Donden's purity of perception, the whole environment appeared to him as a visionary realm. In one place he saw Vajrayoginī and then at Surmang monastery, which was the seat of a special Cakrasaṃvara lineage descended from Tilopa, he saw the symbolic deity, Cakrasaṃvara, and at Dolma Lhakhang, Tārā appeared and inspired Karmapa to compose prayers in her honor. Sachen Kunga Nyingpo, one of the "great five" Sakya *lamas,* appeared to Thongwa Donden in a vision, thereby bringing peace to the many local chiefs who were caught up in fighting.

Karmapa commissioned editions of the *Kanjur* and *Tanjur,* which he paid for with the many offerings he had received on his tours. Throughout this time he continued to receive teachings through visions of Nāgārjuna, the great philosopher, Milarepa and Padmasambhava.

In 1452 Thongwa Donden had presentiments of his imminent death. Lama Sangye Senge offered supplications for his long life and Karmapa said, "This year nothing will happen to me. For the next nine months I shall take responsibility for my life." He went into retreat in the Kongpo area of southern Tibet in preparation for his death.

Karmapa entrusted his books and ceremonial objects to Gyaltshap Gushri Paljor, together with a letter predicting the birth of the next Karmapa incarnation. He said to Gyaltshap Rinpoche, "Until I return, please care for the Kagyu lineage. Now Śambhala[5] and Mecca are at war. I must go to help Śambhala."

Karmapa passed his last months composing songs. At the beginning of 1453, at the age of thirty-seven, he said to his attendants, "I am going to meet the *lamas* of the Kagyu lineage. Learn to recite this supplication: 'I supplicate the great compassionate one, Thongwa Donden. Please regard me with the eye of compassion, embodiment of all the buddhas.'"

He then passed away in meditation. Many relics were discovered in the ashes of the funeral pyre.

Among the sixth Karmapa's principal students were Gyaltshap Gushri Paljor Dondup, Situ Tashi Namgyal and Bengar Jampal Zangpo, to whom he entrusted the lineage.

7
Karmapa Chodrag Gyatsho
(1454–1506)

IN THE FIRST MONTH of 1454 the seventh Karmapa incarnation, Chodrag Gyatsho, was born in northern Tibet. His father was named Drakpa Paldrup and his mother Lhamo Kyi. As a young infant he was recognized to be an incarnation of a spiritual teacher. In his first year he displayed an extraordinary precocity, which confirmed people in this view. One day he spontaneously uttered the seed syllables *āḥ, hūṃ,* and declared, "There is nothing in the world but emptiness. People may think there is substantiality, but they are in error. For me there is neither birth nor death."

The child was taken to the camp of Gyaltshap Paljor Dondrup, the holder of the lineage. Gyaltshap Rinpoche recognized the infant as the new Karmapa incarnation and ceremonially enthroned him. It is said that on this occasion he declared, "I am Vajradhara."

The young Karmapa remained with Gyaltshap Rinpoche and in 1458 at the age of four, made a tour of southern Tibet. As is the case with the Karmapa Lamas, his natural spirituality unfolded through visionary experiences. The young child's innate dignity and presence communicated itself to everyone with whom he came into contact.

As the monastic camp moved through southern Tibet, Chodrag Gyatsho used his influence to stop fighting among Naga and Bhutanese tribes. He also arranged for the freeing of hostages and political prisoners. The young Karmapa was a vegetarian and persuaded many people to give up fishing and hunting. He protected domestic animals, yaks and sheep, and instituted the marking with ribbons to show they were exempt from slaughter. Another aspect of Chodrag Gyatsho's welfare policy was his work to eliminate toll bridges and his construction of iron bridges.

From southern Tibet the camp journeyed slowly into Kham. At Karma monastery, Gyaltshap Rinpoche gave the lay ordination and *bodhisattva* vows to the eight year old Karmapa. The young incarnation's studies continued there and he was subsequently ordained as a novice by Lama Jampal Zangpo, a holder of the lineage and student of the previous Karmapa. His education during this period focused on the *vinaya* texts, dealing with both the general principles and the minutiae of monastic life. Another of the young Karmapa's tutors at this time was Situ Rinpoche, Tashi Namgyal, from whom he received many oral instructions of the Kaṃtshang lineage.

In 1465 Chodrag Gyatsho departed from Karma monastery and traveled to the borderlands of northeastern Tibet. There he brought to an end the feuding of the local Buddhists and Bonpos. In addition to this work in the political sphere, the young Karmapa enunciated the basic message of Buddhism to the local inhabitants. Whatever offerings were made to him on his journey he distributed to the poor and to the monasteries.

Simultaneous with activity for the benefit of others, Chodrag Gyatsho continued his own training. One of the most significant spiritual practices in his career was the *chod* practice from the lineage of the famed *yoginī*, Machig Lab Dronma. While engaged in this meditation the young Karmapa actually saw his own skeleton.

Chodrag Gyatsho was a consummate scholar despite his young age. At Rawa Gang monastery he entered into symposiums and seminars with the five senior scholars. During these seminars Karmapa corrected any inconsistencies in their philosophical viewpoints. At the Surmang monastery of the Trungpa *tulkus*, Chodrag Gyatsho composed several books dealing with various aspects of *dharma*.

In 1471 at the age of seventeen, the seventh Karmapa traveled with his monastic camp to Kawa Karpo, the place of pilgrimage sacred to Cakrasaṃvara. He entered into intensive meditation for seven years there in order to complete his training.

In common with all other Karmapa incarnations, Chodrag Gyatsho had a natural affinity with Guru Padmasambhava. In a certain respect the Karmapa Lama may be considered as an emanation of Padmasambhava. Having returned after his long retreat to Karma Gon monastery, Chodrag Gyatsho had a visionary experience of Guru Padma surrounded by Nyingma symbolic deities, Śākyamuni Buddha and *lamas* of the Kagyu lineage. Karmapa was prompted by this vision to find certain hidden valleys which would afford safety during the coming conflict he foresaw as inevitable.

Subsequently Chodrag Gyatsho revisited southern Tibet, where he repaired several Kagyupa monasteries, and improved their administration. Then he journeyed to Tsurphu, his principal monastery, where he restored the large statue of Śākyamuni, fashioned by Karma Pakshi. Chodrag Gyatsho had made scholarship an important priority. In keeping with this objective, he established a large seminary (Tib.: *shes.'gra*) at Tsurphu, which became very famous.

Karmapa was invited to the court of Tashi Thargye, the Japa Tripon (religio-political ruler) of a province in southern Tibet. Chodrag Gyatsho gave a wide range of Kagyu teachings there and in return Tashi Thargye completely offered his province, fortunes, buildings and monasteries, including his own monastery of Chokhor Lhunpo, to Karmapa. At the court of Tashi Thargye, Chodrag Gyatsho met the first Karma Thinleypa, Cholay Namgyal.[1]

Karma Thinleypa requested Karmapa, whom he regarded as an embodiment of Śākyamuni Buddha, for the secret teachings of the Kagyu lineage. Chodrag Gyatsho replied, "If you promise to hold my lineage I will give my teachings to you." For the next five months Karma Thinleypa studied and practiced the six *yogas* of Nāropa and the *mahāmudrā* until the inner meaning of these teachings was born in him. Chodrag Gyatsho then installed his student as abbot of Chokhor Lhunpo monastery, where he had established a seminary.

The seminary offered a complete course of studies in philosophy, psychology, ritual and religious law. There were three levels of degrees awarded to graduates. At the highest level of proficiency the *khenpo* degree was awarded, followed by that of *lopon* and a pass degree. The seminary, under the direction of Lama Karma Thinleypa played a vital role in the full transmission of Buddhist teaching.

The fame of Chodrag Gyatsho spread as far as India and China. He received offerings from the abbot of Bodhgayā. Several noted Indian scholars, including Rāhula Kīlaya and Śīla Sāgara, came to see Karmapa. From the emperor of China came an invitation to visit. However, Karmapa was unable to go at that time.

In 1498 Chodrag Gyatsho toured the Kongpo area, where he founded a hermitage and recognized the third Situ *tulku,* Tashi Paljor. Following this he returned to Lhasa to hold a religious conference. He was greeted by monks from the Gelugpa monastery of Drepung and Gaden. At Rinpung, Karmapa taught many monks including the great *paṇḍita* Sakya Chokden. His teachings included the *sūtras* and the works of Asaṅga and Nāgārjuna. Chodrag Gyatsho's breadth of scholarship was recognized by members of all the various spiritual traditions.

The seventh Karmapa was a prolific author who composed many texts on *vinaya,* Madhyamaka philosophy, and *tantra.* His assistant, Dakpo Rabjampa Chogyal Tenpa, recorded that when Chodrag Gyatsho worked on a text concerning logic, *Rigjung Jatso,* a commentary of seven books on logic by Dignāga and Dharmakīrti, he dictated it without previous research. He relied on his memory for the sequence of his arguments and for references to the scriptures and commentaries. His stream of thought was unbroken. If his dictation was interrupted he was able to resume it later at the exact point where he had left off. Sometimes his assistant would ask for explanation of an abstruse point, but Karmapa would brush aside the question and it would soon arise naturally in the course of dictation. Occasionally, Chodrag Gyatsho might add, "You should have confidence in what your *guru* says. Explanations will arise later on their own."

Karmapa was very austere and simple in his life-style. Even while traveling he remained silent and mindful. Occasonally he emerged from his seclusion to receive visitors, but when he did so, he never indulged in worldly conversation. In contrast to his own personal austerity Karmapa's monastic camp was richly endowed and beautifully decorated. The shrine tent had a golden roof and was decorated with his most precious relics, above which hung thirteen ornate umbrellas. Chodrag Gyatsho's throne was covered in pearls and behind it was an immense hanging encrusted with pearls.

At the age of fifty-two Karmapa had presentiments of his own imminent death. He advised the Kongpo people to practice *dharma* and then he withdrew into retreat. So many people came to seek an audience with him that Chodrag Gyatsho emerged from retreat and ascended his throne in the shrine tent. He appeared to the people to be garbed in the spiritual apparel of the *sambhogakāya* form. At this time Karmapa transmitted the lineage to Situ Rinpoche and indicated that his next incarnation would be born in Kham and gave the names of his future parents. The next morning Chodrag Gyatsho passed away in meditation.

Karmapa's wealth was divided among Kagyu monasteries. His body was taken to Tsurphu, where it was cremated. Relics, including certain of his bones, were recovered from the pyre and placed in a *stūpa.*

The students of the seventh Karmapa were numerous and included Gyaltshap Tulku, Lama Tashi Namgyal, the fourth Shamar Rinpoche, Lama Sangye Nyenpa, Sakya Choden, Karma Thinleypa, Karma Kachodpa, the logician Wangchuk Gyaltsen, Sakya Wangchuk and the Nyingma *terton,* Samten Lingpa.

8

Karmapa Mikyo Dorje

(1507–1554)

SHORTLY BEFORE HIS DEATH the seventh Karmapa, Chodrag Gyatsho had a visionary experience of Maitreya, the next Buddha, who said, "We are approaching the end of the age of Buddha Śākyamuni and many people are going to lower realms. So you must emanate many incarnations of yourself." In addition, Chodrag Gyatsho foresaw the circumstances of his next birth. On waking the next morning he wrote down the details, which he eventually entrusted to his regent.

On the fourth day of the eleventh month of 1507, the eighth Karmapa, Mikyo Dorje was born in Damchu in eastern Tibet. The new born child opened his eyes and said, "Karmapa."

News of the remarkable child spread quickly and reached the ears of the third Situ Rinpoche, Tashi Paljor, who realized that the child's place of birth agreed with the details left in Chodrag Gyatsho's prediction letter. Situ Rinpoche decided to investigate the child and interviewed the parents. He was satisfied by the similarity between the actual names of Karmapa's parents and those names left in the letter of prediction. In addition, all the other details matched. Situ Rinpoche confirmed that the child was indeed the new incarnation of Karmapa, but asked the parents to maintain absolute secrecy for three months in order to protect the child from unwholesome intrique. He gave the parents some blessing pills, some tea, some butter, and some frankincense and said to them, "Give butter tea to the boy and burn this incense before him, saying that it was sent by Situ Rinpoche. Then give him the blessing pills. If he really is the Karmapa incarnation, he will utter a few words. Tell me what he says."

The father followed these instructions and the infant Karmapa uttered the syllables, *e, ma, ho,* and declared, "Do not doubt me, I am Karmapa." This was reported to Situ Rinpoche, and at the age of three months the young incarnation accompanied him to Karma monastery. Subsequently the child was visited by the great meditation master, Ser Phowa, who had been a close student of the seventh Karmapa. When an offering *pūjā* was performed, the tiny Karmapa played the hand-drum and bell perfectly. Ser Phowa asked him, "If you are Karmapa, do you remember what you taught me in Tse Lhakhang?" The boy replied, "I gave you *mahāmudrā* and the six doctrines of Nāropa."

In 1512, at the age of five, Mikyo Dorje journeyed to Riwoche. There he was asked by Lama Sonam Rinchen to say who he really was. The boy laughed and declared, "Sometimes I am Padmasambhava, sometimes Saraha and at other times I am Karmapa. I have many emanations. In Tsang province there are sixteen, and west of Tibet there is a chieftain who is my emanation."

In the same year a young boy from the region of Amdo was put forward as a rival claimant to be the new Karmapa incarnation. Gyaltshap Rinpoche set out to investigate the rival's claims but when he met Mikyo Dorje, he spontaneously felt compelled to bow down to him. Realizing this boy was the Karmapa incarnation, Gyaltshap Rinpoche sent letters of authority to all Karma Kagyu monasteries in which he declared that, according to a prediction by Padmasambhava, the name of the eighth Karmapa was Mikyo Dorje. In the following year, Gyaltshap Rinpoche ceremonially enthroned the young boy as the eighth Karmapa at Tse Lhakhang.

The education of the eighth Karmapa commenced when he reached the age of seven. His first tutor was Situ Rinpoche, from whom he received the eight moral precepts[1] and some elementary Kagyu teachings. Then Mikyo Dorje set out on a tour of monasteries. At Surmang monastery a vision of the Kagyu lineage evoked in him a realization of the richness of his inheritance. A little later the young Karmapa met with the meditation master Sangye Nyenpa, whom Chodrag Gyatsho had appointed as the transmitter of the lineage to his next incarnation.

Following this initial meeting, Mikyo Dorje and his camp traveled into far Kham. The unfoldment of his inner potential was continued by a visionary experience in which he received teachings from Śākyamuni Buddha accompanied by his two chief students, Śāriputra and Mahāmaudgalyāyana. While in this area, the young Karmapa incarnation had a very significant dream in which a *ḍākinī* told him, "You are the activity aspect of the buddhas of the three times."

Mikyo Dorje and his party returned briefly to Riwoche, where he carried out both religious and welfare work. Afterward Karmapa revisited the area of his birth in Damchu province. There he had a profound visionary experience in which Guru Padmasambhava revealed to him his true nature, saying, "I am Padmasambhava and you are my principal student, Gyalwa Choyang.[2] The unity of our two natures is Vajradhara."

A short time after this, Mikyo Dorje, inspired by the memory of Dusum Khyenpa, made a pilgrimage to Kampo Gangra. It is said that he left footprints in the various meditation caves there.

In 1516 the nine year old Karmapa received an invitation from the king of Jang Sa-tham. The invitation was accepted, and Mikyo Dorje, accompanied by his camp, set out. The party was welcomed with great ceremony on its arrival and the king lavished honor and offerings on the young Karmapa. The uncontrived dignity of Mikyo Dorje made a deep impact on the king, who had previously not been well disposed to Buddhism. He made provision for the support of the *dharma* in his territories and also undertook to adopt a policy of nonaggression in political matters. Before leaving, Mikyo Dorje promised to return in seven years.

In 1517 the young Karmapa entered into the most important phase of his education. During the next three years he received, from Lama Sangye Nyenpa, a thorough grounding in a comprehensive range of Buddhist teachings, in addition to the complete transmission of the Karma Kagyu lineage. Despite his wealth, Sangye Nyenpa was a perfect example of Kagyu asceticism. At the conclusion of this three year period of teaching he died, without regret, in the knowledge that Mikyo Dorje had absorbed his instructions. During the funeral ceremonies, Karmapa experienced the presence of his deceased guru and received absolute clarification of his teachings.

Mikyo Dorje was similar to the third Karmapa in his appetite for learning and scholarship. He was a very talented linguist and mastered Sanskrit grammar under the direction of Lotsawa Richen Tashi. The eighth Karmapa also ventured into the fields of poetry, painting and sculpture, where he met with considerable success. As a monk Mikyo Dorje was an example of austerity and simplicity. As a master of *mahāmudrā* he lived in the realization that whatever arises is self-liberated.

In one of his visions, a monk appeared to Mikyo Dorje announcing that he had been Padmasambhava during the age of the previous Buddha, Dīpaṃkara. Mikyo Dorje responded with a question, "If this is so, where was your 'lotus birth' and where did you stay?" The monk replied, "Where did space come from?" He then disappeared. Reflecting on this, Karmapa realized that each of the thousand buddhas is accompanied by a Padmasambhava as a natural expression of the teaching of enlightenment.

Subsequently Mikyo Dorje and his great camp traveled slowly through Kham, where he gave teachings to more than ten thousand people. During this tour he recognized the third Gyaltshap *tulku,* Drakpa Paljor, and the fifth Shamar Rinpoche, Konchog Yenlag. At Mar Kham, Mikyo Dorje carved a statue of himself out of stone. It is recorded that he placed the statue in front of him and asked it, "Are you a good likeness of me?" The statue replied, "Yes, I am." Then Karmapa squeezed a chunk of left-over stone like a piece of butter, leaving the imprint of his palm and fingers in it. Both the statue and the stone have been preserved and are now at the residence of the present Karmapa at Rumtek monastery in Sikkim.

On his arrival at Karma monastery, Mikyo Dorje met emissaries of the Chinese Emperor Wu Tsung, who presented him with many invitation offerings and on behalf of the emperor, invited him to China. However, Karmapa foresaw the emperor's imminent death and declined the invitation. The Chinese envoys took offence at this and repacking the emperor's offerings to Karmapa, returned to China, where they discovered that the empress and emperor had just died.

From Kham, Mikyo Dorje traveled to central Tibet. At Saṃding, the Dorje Phagmo *tulku* made the offering of a monastery to him. On reaching Tsurphu, he found it was in a state of disrepair and arranged for restoration work to be carried out. Karmapa was visited by Surmang Trungpa Tulku, who saw him as the embodiment of Cakrasaṃvara.

After a period of administrative work Mikyo Dorje set out again with his retinue. He visited the Kadampa monastery of Radeng. From there he went on to Gangri Thokar, the retreat of the great Nyingma saint, Longchenpa, where he left his footprints and the hoofprints of his horse in the rock.

From there Mikyo Dorje journeyed to where the aged Lama Karma Thinley was in retreat. Karma Thinleypa gave Karmapa the empowerments of Kurukullā, Mahākāla and Vaiśravaṇa. Then together they went to Karma Thinleypa's doctrinal school (Tib.: *shes.'gra*) at Lekshay Ling, where Mikyo Dorje gave many teachings.

Later in the following year Karmapa met Lama Karma Thinley again. This time the venerable scholar instructed Mikyo Dorje in the six doctrines of Nāropa. At the age of twenty-one, Karmapa was ordained a monk by the abbot, Chodrup Senge, who was an incarnation of the Kashmiri scholar, Śākyaśrī. The abbot was assisted at the ceremony by Lama Karma Thinley.

At this time Chodrup Senge gave Mikyo Dorje very detailed teachings on the "empty of something else view" (Tib.: *gzhan.stong.lta.ba*). He asked Mikyo Dorje to promulgate this vitally important philosophical concept, which had gained wide currency in the Jonangpa and Nyingma traditions. It had been attacked by adherents of the Gelugpa tradition, who held the opposing view, "empty of selfness view" (Tib.: *rang.stong.lta.ba*). The "empty of something else view" was passed down through the lineage and reached the fifteenth Karmapa through Jamgon Kongtrul Lodro Thaye. Kongtrul Rinpoche made this view the cornerstone of his Rime ("boundaryless") approach. Thus, Mikyo Dorje may be seen as an important precursor of this nineteenth century Buddhist renaissance.

Mikyo Dorje's relationship with Je Karma Thinleypa was of great importance in his training. He stayed with him, in all, for three years. During this period he studied the *Five Books of Maitreya,* Dignāga and Dharmakīrti's texts on logic, the *abhidharma* (Skt.: *Abhidharmasamuccaya*) of Asaṅga and the *abhidharma* (Skt.: *Abhidharmakośa*) of Vasubandhu, the *vinaya* texts, the six principal texts of Nāgārjuna, Candrakīrti's *Entering into the Middle Way* (Skt.: *Madhyamakāvatāra*), the *Hevajra Tantra,* astrology and many other Indian works on the *mahāyāna* and *vajrayāna* approaches to Buddhism. In addition to the wide ranging study of Indian Buddhism, Karma Thinleypa introduced Mikyo Dorje to the collected works of Ngok Lotsawa[4] and Sakya Paṇḍita.

Mikyo Dorje was an exemplary student, maintaining complete mindfulness throughout this long and intense period of study. He constantly reflected on the meaning of the texts and whatever points arose from them. He questioned and debated all abstruse points and in this manner developed a perfect realization. Karmapa studied so much he had little time to eat, and as a result his physical strength weakened. Thinleypa praised Karmapa as a great scholar. In return Mikyo Dorje praised his tutor, saying, "You are on the first *bodhisattva* level, the border of *saṃsāra* and *nirvāṇa.* As far as *saṃsāra* is concerned, you are a nonreturner and you have the power of incarnation."

At the conclusion of his intellectual studies Mikyo Dorje devoted more of his time to meditation. In a visionary experience, *ḍākinīs* carried him into the presence of the *mahāsiddha,* Śavaripa, who had transmitted the *mahāmudrā* to Maitrīpa. Savaripa then introduced Mikyo Dorje to the nature of his own mind, saying, "Both *saṃsāra* and *nirvāṇa* come from mind. Your own mind is itself wisdom. So there are no different levels. Everything comes from mind." Then the *mahāsiddha* disappeared.

Mikyo Dorje himself became a very prolific author whose works were both controversial and influential. At the age of twenty-three he wrote a commentary on the *Abhisamayālaṅkāra* entitled, *Authentic Relaxation of the Noble One* (Tib.: *rje.btsun.ngal.so*). He then invited the Gelugpa scholar, Sera Jetsun, to a critical debate on the text. This talented scholar responded by composing a commentary of his own in which he wrote, "Karmapa is a high incarnation and scholar. Therefore, I am unable to criticize him. However, at his invitation I am following his commentary with my own book entitled, *A Reply to Karmapa.*" In this way a famous literary debate took place between the brilliant Karmapa and the famous Gelugpa scholar.

Mikyo Dorje authored over thirty volumes in all, fourteen more than Karma Pakshi. These included texts on linguistics, religious law, *abhidharma, tantra,* Madhyamaka philosophy, art and poetry. He composed important texts on *mahāmudrā* and inspired the Karma Gadri movement in art through his work in this field. In addition he composed the spiritual practice known as *The Guru Yoga of the Four Sessions* (Tib.: *thun.bzhi. bla.ma'i.rnal.'byor*) in honor of his *guru* Sangye Nyenpa. This has become one of the most important practices of the Kaṃtshang lineage.

In 1546 Mikyo Dorje had a premonition of his imminent death. However, Shamar Rinpoche and Pawo Rinpoche entreated their *guru* to remain and continue his work. Responding to their request Karmapa agreed to extend his life span for several years. He set out with his monastic camp on a long final tour of Karma Kagyupa monasteries and *dharma* centers. On this tour Mikyo Dorje told his officials to relax the normally strict protocol that surrounded him. It was his wish that it be as easy as possible for people to have an audience with him.

While traveling, Mikyo Dorje wrote many poetic accounts of his visionary experiences. One of the most significant was one in which he envisaged Cakrasaṃvara seated above the head of Vajrayoginī. From the *guru,* in the form of Cakrasaṃvara, came the nectar of wisdom, which transformed the concepts of *saṃsāra* and *nirvāṇa* into wisdom of enlightenment. A *vajra* hook made the wisdom unshakeable. Then in the same vision he saw *saṃsāra* burned away in a cooking pot, which rested on a *vajra* trivet. In another visionary experience Mikyo Dorje saw eight Padmasambhavas and eight Karmapas combine to produce a secret teaching.

In his final years Mikyo Dorje's health declined, but despite this he continued his arduous work unabated. In 1554 there was an outbreak of leprosy in southern Tibet. Karmapa traveled there in an effort to bring the epidemic to an end. He had a black *stūpa* surrounded by four smaller *stūpas* constructed in the center of the area. The central *stūpa* was a symbolic representation of a *nāga* ("snake spirit"), which in myth was said to cause leprosy. The four surrounding *stūpas* symbolized its arms and legs. Then Mikyo Dorje went into the center of the area and with the power of his compassion absorbed the imbalance that was causing the disease into himself. The epidemic quickly cleared and Mikyo Dorje returned to the Dakpo Shedrup Ling monastery of Shamar Rinpoche.

However, a little while later, Karmapa himself began to exhibit signs of leprosy and was soon unable to walk. He realized the imminence of his own death and so he arrayed himself in the dress and ornaments of the *sambhogakāya,* the communicative form of buddhahood, and showed himself in this manner to his students. Subsequently Mikyo Dorje entrusted Shamar Rinpoche with the letters containing the predictions of his next rebirth, and passed away at the age of forty-seven. His corpse was cremated at Tsurphu. Shamar Rinpoche enshrined his relics in a silver *stūpa.*

The eighth Karmapa had many accomplished and scholarly students. Among the most outstanding were Shamar Konchog Yenlag, Pawo Tsuglak Tengwa, Gyaltshap Drakpa Paljor, Situ Chokyi Gocha and Karma Thinley Legdrup. He also numbered artists, doctors and poets among his disciples, on whom he exerted a profound influence.

9

Karmapa Wangchuk Dorje

(1555–1603)

THE NINTH KARMAPA, Wangchuk Dorje, was born in the seventh month of 1555. It is recorded that immediately after his birth he wiped his face three times and declared, "I am Karmapa." The infant quickly became famous and reports of him reached Situ Rinpoche at Karma monastery. Since the circumstances of the birth coincided with the details contained in a prediction written down by Mikyo Dorje in his twenty-eighth year, Situ Rinpoche dispatched two assistants to investigate the infant. The assistants reported that they were satisfied that the child was indeed Karmapa. Situ Rinpoche then informed the officials of Tsurphu monastery that the new Karmapa incarnation had been discovered.

The small black hat, the seal, the robes and some ritual implements of the Karmapas were sent from Tsurphu to Karma monastery. The boy correctly identified a bell, which had belonged to Chodrag Gyatsho, the seventh Karmapa. The following year, Shamar Konchog Yenlag conveyed the ritual objects entrusted to him by Mikyo Dorje. At about the same time, the political authorities in central Tibet sent letters of authority recognizing the new Karmapa incarnation. This last move reflected the secular power's awareness of the political importance of the Karmapa at this time. Increasingly the various schools were being brought willingly or unwillingly into the political arena. This was an important trend during the troubled life-times of the next three Karmapas.

At the age of six, Wangchuk Dorje was ceremonially enthroned by Shamar Rinpoche. He also received refuge and *bodhisattva* vows and the empowerment of Amitāyus as well as many other textual transmissions, empowerments and teachings. Shamarpa continued to teach the young Karmapa, giving him the textual transmission of texts from the *Tripiṭaka* and certain Kagyupa texts. During this time Karmapa's monastic camp journeyed slowly to Tsurphu. On the way Wangchuk Dorje accompanied Shamar Rinpoche in pilgrimage to Kampo Nenang, where Dusum Khyenpa had meditated.

The journey continued through Surmang and Nangchen, arriving at Tsurphu in the new year period of 1561. In his first public teaching, Wangchuk Dorje taught the four *dharmas* of Gampopa[1] to eighteen hundred monks and many political representatives of central Tibet. Then, accompanied by Shamarpa and Pawo Rinpoche, the young Karmapa undertook a pilgrimage to southern Tibet. The camp stopped at Lekshay Ling monastery, where Wangchuk Dorje honored the enshrined remains of the first Karma Thinleypa. From there they traveled into Lhodrak, the home of Marpa, the father of the Kagyu lineage. Pawo Rinpoche assisted Shamar Rinpoche in performing the novice ordination for the young Karmapa. His two tutors also began to instruct him in the teachings of *mahāmudrā* and the six doctrines of Nāropa.

The greater part of Wangchuk Dorje's childhood was spent traveling with his camp. This nomadic monastery was very strict in its discipline and the intensity of practice. The scholars among Karmapa's entourage concentrated upon the study of the *Hevajra Tantra* and the *Cakrasaṃvara Tantra,* the *Uttaratantra Śāstra* of Maitreya, and the *Zabmo Nangdon* of Rangjung Dorje. The advanced *tantric* practitioners of the monastic camp practiced the six *yogas* of Nāropa, *mahāmudrā* and *chod.* The camp's ordinary practitioners and monks meditated upon Vajrayoginī, Avalokiteśvara and Hayagrīva. In order to be fully accepted into Karmapa's entourage at this time, a follower had to have accomplished a great amount of spiritual practice.

At Shamar Rinpoche's monastery of Yangbachen, Wangchuk Dorje instructed the monks in various teachings. He spent three months at the court of the local prince in Rinpung, Ngawang Jigten Wangchuk. He received a visit there from Lama Sonam Gyatsho, the then head of the Gelugpa sect. Sonam Gyatsho later received the title of Dalai Lama ("Ocean Guru") from the Mongol, Aarten Khan.

Wangchuk Dorje next journeyed through the Kongpo province in southern Tibet, which had always been a stronghold of the Kaṃtshang and Drukpa Kagyu. Shamarpa instructed him in the teachings of Rangjung Dorje and Mikyo Dorje as they traveled.

In addition to his studies, Wangchuk Dorje was called upon to mediate and arbitrate local disputes. Having moved the camp south to Tsari,

Karmapa received a second visit from Sonam Gyatsho, who requested him to mediate a political dispute in the Yarlung principality. Together, the two *lamas* brought about a three year treaty and then parted after an exchange of gifts.

In 1580 Wangchuk Dorje received the final ordination from Shamar Rinpoche. Subsequently, he studied the *vinaya* and then the teaching of the fifth, sixth and seventh Karmapas. As well as these Kaṃtshang Kagyu teachings, Karmapa also received textual transmissions of texts from the Drigung Kagyu and Kadampa lineages from Shamar Rinpoche.

In 1583 Shamar Rinpoche passed away. Wangchuk Dorje enshrined his *guru's* remains in a *stūpa* at Yangbachen monastery. He undertook to divide Shamarpa's property among the monasteries at U and Tsang, giving gifts and tea to poor people and a gold *maṇḍala* to the great temple at Lhasa. After a pilgrimage to sacred places in northern Tibet, Wangchuk Dorje returned to Tsurphu, where he transmitted the texts of Mikyo Dorje and the Drigung Kagyu tradition to Pawo *tulku.* He also ordained many monks at this time and ordered the completion of an enormous silk applique *thangka* of Buddha Śākyamuni.

It was then necessary for Wangchuk Dorje to travel to Rinpung, where he settled some political difficulties. Karmapa was saddened by the political troubles of his time. He felt that the memory of the early period of Buddhism in Tibet would inspire a renewed dedication to the civilizing messages of *dharma.* In pursuit of this aim he arranged for the repair of temples built by the earlier Buddhist kings, Srongtsen Gampo and Trisong Detsun.

After ordaining the third Pawo *tulku,* Tsuglak Gyatsho, Karmapa entered into retreat for a year at Tsurphu. Then he set out on a tour of northern Tibet, where it was said that the king of the Nāgas made an offering to him, symbolizing the dedication of the area of Karmapa. People attributed that year's good weather and harvests to this offering.

Although not as prolific an author as the previous Karmapa, Wangchuk Dorje composed some important texts, including a commentary on the Drigung "one thought" viewpoint. His most important book was *The Ocean of Certainty* (Tib.: *nges.don.rgya.mtsho*), from which has come the liturgy of the preliminary practices of *mahāmudrā.* Another important work of the ninth Karmapa was entitled, *Eliminating the Darkness of Ignorance* (Tib.: *ma.rigs.dmun.bsal*) and this was also concerned with *mahāmudrā.* Both are in current use today.

Wangchuk Dorje engaged extensively in work in both the religious and social spheres. At Ngakphu he ordained many monks among the local people. He also stopped hunting and fishing and tried to inculcate in the local people an attitude of reverence toward animals. In addition, Karmapa arranged for the construction of bridges in the area.

A little later, word reached Wangchuk Dorje that the new Shamar incarnation had been born in a Drigung family. He recognized the child as the incarnation and, at about this time, also ordained a large number of Drigungpa monks. In 1594 Karmapa took the infant Shamarpa back to Tsurphu where he began to instruct him in the Kaṃtshang tradition.

Wangchuk Dorje next journeyed with his monastic camp to Tsari. There he taught Vajrayoginī meditation to those practitioners, who were on retreat. He also gave the textual transmission of Gampopa's collected works and ordained many monks.

Karmapa's camp traveled to Kongpo, passing through Gampopa's old monastery of Dak Lha Gampo. In Kongpo, Wangchuk Dorje distributed aid to the local people and contributed funds for the upkeep of the temples. His stay in the Kongpo area lasted for eight years, alternating between periods of activity and retreat. An especially important aspect of Karmapa's practice in retreat was meditation on Mahākāla. In teaching, Wangchuk Dorje emphasized the texts of the eight Karmapas.

Wangchuk Dorje established a new retreat center at Tashi Gungtang, where the third Karmapa, Rangjung Dorje, had meditated. While he was there, Wangchuk Dorje composed commentaries on the *Kālacakra Tantra* and the four grades of *tantra.* He also wrote a *sādhana* of Vairocana. He completed the textual transmission of the texts of the eight Karmapas, which he had begun earlier, and then led a "wish-prayer festival." Finally, after bestowing the empowerment of Kālacakra on his camp, Karmapa went back into retreat.

At the conclusion of this period of intensive practice, Wangchuk Dorje instructed his students in the quintessential Kagyupa teachings. He began by teaching Gampopa's *Jewel Ornament of Liberation,* in which is set out the graduated path by which the student enters into *dharma* and progresses through the *hīnayāna* and *mahāyāna* levels to enlightenment. Then Wangchuk Dorje gave teachings on the *vajrayāna* level, emphasizing the six doctrines of Nāropa and the *mahāmudrā.* Subsequently, to transmit the inspiration of his lineage, Karmapa performed the black crown ceremony for ten thousand people. He then ordained the fifth Situ Rinpoche, Chokyi Gyaltsen, and instructed him in Kagyupa doctrine.

The ninth Karmapa received invitations from the Mongol authorities in China but declined them. However, he did consent to visit U and Tsang. Wangchuk Dorje traveled to the head Drukpa Kagyu monastery, Sang Ngag Choling, where he gave teachings. Before returning to Tsurphu, Karmapa visited many places in Tsang and the Rinpung area. Wangchuk Dorje celebrated the new year "wish-prayer" festival with his camp and ordained the sixth Shamar *tulku,* Chokyi Wangchuk, at that time.

Karmapa took a large interest in the restoration and improvement of Kagyupa monasteries. He requested the second Lama Karma Thinleypa to repair the Shedrup Ling monastery. Karma Thinley was able to fulfill Wangchuk Dorje's wishes.

Karmapa traveled to Outer Mongolia at the request of the King Hortu. In honor of Wangchuk Dorje's compassionate message, the king freed all condemned prisoners and vowed to observe nonviolence. Karmapa performed the ceremony of the *vajra* crown and instructed the court and the people in the development of awakened compassion through the meditation of Avalokiteśvara.

One of the ninth Karmapa's most influential students was the prolific Jonangpa scholar and translator, Tāranātha, who wrote the *History of Dharma in India.* Wangchuk Dorje gave him all the empowerments, textual transmissions and instructions of the Karma Kagyu lineage. During his teaching, Karmapa took a bowl of barley, stirred it with a whip, and placed it on Tāranātha's head, saying, "As Karma Pakshi did to Urgyenpa, so do I to you. I give you the whole transmission of the Kagyu lineage."

Just after the new year's festival of 1603, Karmapa began to feel unwell. He realized death was imminent and gave letters predicting his new rebirth in Kham. He died the following morning. His remains were enshrined at Tsurphu.

The principal students of Wangchuk Dorje were, Shamar Chokyi Wangchuk, Lotsawa Tāranātha, Situ Chokyi Gyaltsen, Pawo Tsuglak Gyatsho, Drigung Kagyupa Chokyi Rinchen Namgyal and Taglung Kagyupa Chokyi Kunga Tashi.

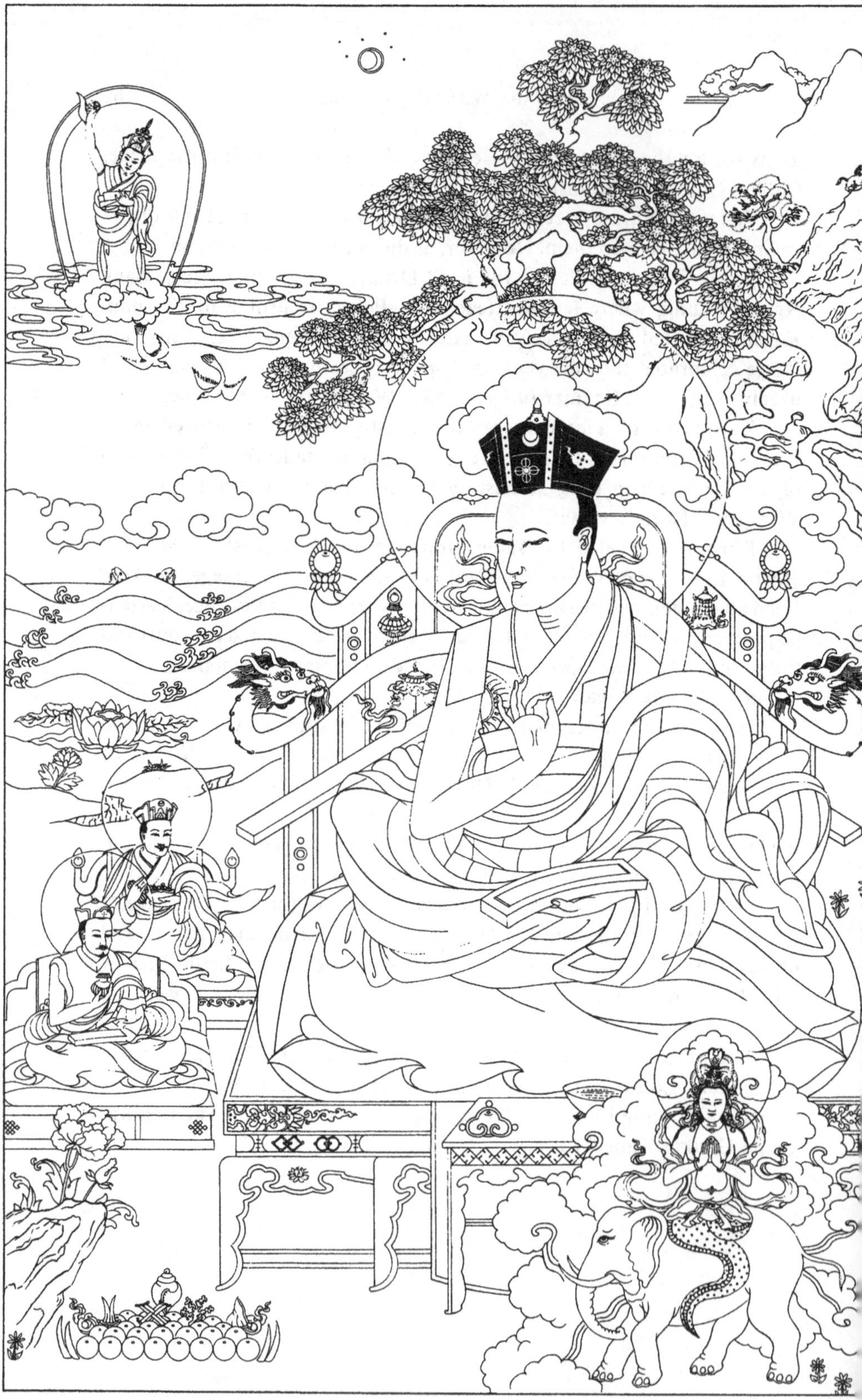

10
Karmapa Choying Dorje
(1604–1674)

THE TENTH KARMAPA, Choying Dorje, was born on the eighth day of the third month of Wood Dragon year (1604 C.E.) in the Golok area of eastern Tibet. His mother had had auspicious dreams of Guru Padmasambhava during her pregnancy and so she named her baby Urgyen Khyab ("protected by the one from Urgyen").

It is recorded that at birth the infant stood up and took one step in each direction as Śākyamuni Buddha had done at his birth. He then sat down crossed-legged and was heard to recite the *mantra* of Avalokiteśvara and that of the "perfection of wisdom."[1]

Choying Dorje spent his early childhood in the palace of the local prince, Chang Mowa, at Machu, where he was feted as a remarkable prodigy. He showed an exceptional ability in art, an ability which came to fruition in later life. The young Karmapa demonstrated a great natural tenderness toward animals. The sight, one day, of sheep being shorn caused the young child to burst into tears and beg the shearers not to harm them. On another occasion he gave protection to a hunted deer and then tamed the hunting dog that was pursuing it. When the hunter arrived, Karmapa provided him with funds to start a new livelihood and as a result the hunter renounced killing.

The young Karmapa had a lively and playful sense of humor. On one occasion he was seated on a horse in front of his father held between his father's arms. He asked his father to give him the reins so that he could direct the horse. The young boy spontaneously made up a little song saying that people should not travel lazily but that everyone should lead themselves to enlightenment.

At the age of eight Choying Dorje was officially recognized as the Karmapa incarnation by the sixth Shamar Rinpoche. Subsequently Shamarpa ceremonially enthroned Choying Dorje at Nyingche Ling monastery. Karmapa envisaged the glorious *dharmapāla,* Mahākāla, at this ceremony, which was a very joyous and auspicious event. A few days afterwards Choying Dorje was walking with some monks on the banks of the Dzachu River, when he remarked on a large rock in midstream. He asked some of the monks to bring it out and split it in half. The rock was very difficult to move but Karmapa said that it must be done for the benefit of sentient beings. When the rock was finally broken in half, it was found to contain many green worms wriggling in agony. With great tenderness for their hellish suffering, Choying Dorje recited Avalokiteśvara's *mantra.* They gradually became still and passed away peacefully.

A little later Choying Dorje journeyed to Tsurphu. After his arrival in Tsurphu, Karmapa met Pawo Tsuglak Gyatsho, from whom he received lay ordination and the empowerments, textual transmissions and instructions of Karma Pakshi, Rangjung Dorje and Chodrag Gyatsho.

The political climate during the boyhood of the tenth Karmapa was steadily worsening. After his period of study with Pawo Rinpoche, Karmapa was invited to the court of the prince of Tsang, Karma Phuntsog Namgyal, who subsequently extended his rule throughout Tibet after the fall of the Rinpung dynasty.

This prince was a patron of the Kaṃtshang Kagyu and Drukpa Kagyu. He asked Choying Dorje to pray for peace because he was threatened by a marauding Mongol chief. This time the invasion was averted.

Choying Dorje's education resumed at Tsurphu, where Pawo Rinpoche gave him the complete transmission of Kagyu *dharma.* At the age of twenty-one he was ordained a monk. He then entered into intensive meditation on the teaching he had received.

Later, traveling with Shamar Rinpoche, Situ Rinpoche, and Pawo Rinpoche, Choying Dorje visited Lhodrag, where he was informed of the death of the prince of Tsang. The deceased prince's wife asked Karmapa to perform the death rites for her husband. For that purpose the party then traveled to Lhasa and the palace of Samdrup Ling.

At the conclusion of this period Karmapa made a pilgrimage to the original Nyingma monastery of Samye, where Shamar Rinpoche gave him the *bodhisattva* vows. From there Choying Dorje continued on his pilgrimage visiting the caves of Padmasambhava and Milarepa and Mount Kailāsa. At Chuwar, the scene of Milarepa's decease, Karmapa established a meditation center. Subsequently, he traveled on to Daklha Gampo monastery. There he painted a large golden mural of the sixteen *arhats* and their followers. At about this time, Shamar Rinpoche became ill and passed away.

The political trouble that had erupted in Tsang as a result of the animosity felt toward the monasteries of Sera and Drepung by the king of Tsang, Desi Karma Tenkyong Wangpo, precipitated a Mongol invasion which spread rapidly throughout Tibet. Choying Dorje moved ahead of it to Jang Sa-tham, the Sino-Tibetan border region, where King Karma Chimed Lawang and his court received him with honor. In virtual exile, Karmapa devoted his time to instructing the people in Karma Kagyu Buddhism, helping the poor and aiding the temples of the locality.

While Choying Dorje was occupied in this way the army of Jang won a victory over a marauding splinter force of three hundred thousand soldiers and prepared to send them against the main Mongol army in Tibet itself, led by Gushri Khan, a supporter of the Gelugpa school. When Choying Dorje was informed of this plan, he told the king that to engage in such a military venture was contrary to the nonviolent ethic of *dharma.* He dissuaded the king from this course of action, saying, "I am committed not to arm even tiny insects, so do not send an army." Karmapa was successful and the king called off the mobilization.

Having resolved this political difficulty, Choying Dorje continued his *dharma* activity by establishing a new monastery named Ogmin Ling. He also ordained many monks and gave a textual transmission of the *Tripiṭaka* texts. While teaching at this time, Karmapa had a premonition of the rebirth of Shamar Rinpoche. Immediately he set out by himself from Jang Sa-tham to search for the new Shamarpa. He disguised himself as a beggar, so that he would be able to travel unhindered through the troubled land. Finally, on arrival in the Golok region, Choying Dorje met a child whom he recognized to be the new incarnation of Shamar Rinpoche. It is recorded that the young incarnation had no difficulty in recognizing Karmapa despite the latter's disguise. At Suchu Karpo, Choying Dorje gave refuge and some preliminary teachings of the Kagyupa tradition to the young Shamar Yeshe Nyingpo.

While traveling in Golok, Choying Dorje recognized and enthroned the new incarnation of the Gyaltshap *tulku.* Subsequently he met the new incarnations of the Situ and Pawo Rinpoches in Kham. After giving the young incarnations some preliminary teachings, Karmapa, together with his party, left Jang for Lhasa after having been away for thirty years.

During this time he met Tulku Minjur Dorje, who was a student of Chagmed Rāga-asi Rinpoche, an emanation of Mikyo Dorje and founder of the Nedo subsect of the Karma Kagyu. Karmapa recognized Minjur Dorje's *terma* ("treasure text") teaching,[2] which derived from the inspiration of Guru Padmasambhava, as authentic. In response Minjur Dorje offered his *termas* to Choying Dorje. In the Karma Kagyu sect, Minjur Dorje's most renowned teaching has been his *sādhana* of Karma Pakshi.

In the Water Ox year Choying Dorje arrived in Lhasa. Immediately upon his arrival, he extended an invitation to the fifth Dalai Lama, Ngawang Lobzang Gyatsho, who welcomed him and expressed his appreciation that the Jang army was not going to invade Tibet. During their meeting, Ngawang Lobzang Gyatsho and Choying Dorje discussed *mahāmudrā,* and Karmapa was assured that Tsurphu would be given protection in case of need.

From Lhasa, Karmapa visited the birthplace of Yeshe Tsogyal, the consort of Guru Padmasambhava. His party visited the famous lake that was said to have appeared at the time of her birth, and also some of Padmasambhava's meditation caves.

Finally Choying Dorje returned to Tsurphu, after his years of wandering. In 1673 he received intimations of his approaching death in a vision of Mahākālī. He entrusted the details of his next rebirth with his servant Kuntu Zangpo, with Shamar Rinpoche and with Gyaltshap Rinpoche. At dawn on the full moon day of the second month of the Wood Tiger year, Choying Dorje passed away at the age of seventy. His remains were enshrined in a *stūpa,* which was placed with those of the previous Karmapas in Tsurphu.

The tenth Karmapa's principal students were Shamar Yeshe Nyingpo, Gyaltshap Drakpa Choying, Kuntu Zangpo, Situ Mipham Thinley Rabten, Pawo Thinley Gyatsho, Karma Chagmed Rāga-asi Rinpoche, the famous Nyingma *terton* Jatson Nyingpo, the king of Jang Sa-tham, Karma Tsewang Rinchen, Prince Karma Rinchen who achieved the path of vision and the joyful stage, Prince Karma Phuntsok, the Prime Minister Karma Tenkyong, treasurer Karma Samdrup, Taklung Ngawang Tashi Paldrup, Surmang Garwang Rinchen Nyingpo and the fourth Surmang Trungpa Tulku.

11

Karmapa Yeshe Dorje

(1676–1702)

THE ELEVENTH KARMAPA, Yeshe Dorje, was born in Mar Kham in the year of the Fire Dragon (1676 C.E.). The young child had many visionary experiences that he liked to relate to his relatives, much to their amusement. This amusement gradually turned to awe as they realized the natural dignity of these stories and the spirituality of the infant.

The famed *terton,* Minjur Dorje, who was a master of both Kagyu and Nyingma sects recognized the child as the Karmapa incarnation. News of this traveled and Shamar Rinpoche and Gyaltshap Rinpoche sent their representatives, who confirmed that the details of Yeshe Dorje's birth corresponded to those in the letters of prediction. At Dechen Yangbachen, the monastery of Shamar Rinpoche, the new Karmapa was given a great ceremonial welcome. Then he was taken to Tsurphu, where he was enthroned by Shamar Yeshe Nyingpo.

After receiving lay ordination[1] from Shamar Rinpoche, Yeshe Dorje commenced his studies. His tutors included Shamar Rinpoche, Gyaltshap Rinpoche and the third Karma Thinleypa. Yeshe Dorje received the complete lineage transmission of the Kagyupa tradition. It was at this time that he was given the name Yeshe Dorje by Terton Minjur Dorje, who related Padmasambhava's prediction concerning the eleventh Karmapa.

On the death of Shamar Yeshe Nyingpo, the young Karmapa went to study with Terton Minjur Dorje and Taksham Nuden Dorje, a Nyingmapa *terton.* These two meditation masters instructed Yeshe Dorje in their "treasure texts."

During Yeshe Dorje's youth in the year of the Water Dog, the fifth Dalai Lama died. Rule was assumed by Desi Sangye Gyatsho, the Dalai Lama's regent, who continued the policy of reconciliation. One of the most influential figures in the exchange between the Gelugpas and the Karma

Kagyupas at this time was Tewo Rinpoche, Karma Tendzin Thargye, who had served the fifth Dalai Lama and was one of the principal students of Karmapa Yeshe Dorje.

In the year of the Wooden Pig, Yeshe Dorje had a vision that indicated that the eighth Shamar Rinpoche had been born in Nepal near Jomo Gangkar mountain. Karmapa's representatives located the child and returned with him to Tsurphu. The party passed through Lhasa with the permission of Desi Sangye Gyatsho. After the young incarnation's arrival at Tsurphu, he was enthroned by Karmapa and received the red crown of the Shamarpa incarnation lineage. Subsequently, Yeshe Dorje recognized the new incarnations of the Situ and Pawo Rinpoches, respectively, Tenpi Nyinche and Chokyi Dondrup.

Yeshe Dorje's consummate spirituality communicated itself both through his teaching and the apparently miraculous quality of his activity. On one occasion Karmapa demonstrated the power of his teaching by emanating several forms of himself, each of which gave instruction to the individuals present.

The eleventh Karmapa was the shortest lived of the Karmapa incarnations. In 1702 he entrusted a letter containing a prediction of his next rebirth to Shamar Rinpoche, whom he appointed his regent. A little later, Yeshe Dorje passed away at age twenty-six. At the time of Karmapa's death many of his students saw his form appear in front of the sun, accompanied by the figures of two other gurus. Yeshe Dorje's remains were enshrined in a *stūpa* at Tsurphu monastery.

The eleventh Karmapa's principal students were the eighth Shamar, Palchen Chokyi Dondrup, and Tewo Rinpoche, Karma Tendzin Thargye.

12

Karmapa Changchub Dorje

(1703–1732)

THE TWELFTH KARMAPA, Changchub Dorje, was born in the Dege area of Kham in the year of the Water Sheep (1703 C.E.). In accordance with the letter of prediction left by the pervious Karmapa, his birthplace was beside the Golden River (Yangtse). Shortly before his birth his father, who was the owner of a pottery business, had been told by Terton Minjur Dorje that an auspicious event was about to occur in his family. Changchub Dorje's family was, in fact, descended from that of King Trisong Detsun.

When he was two months old, Changchub Dorje was heard to declare, "I am the Karmapa." News of this and of Minjur Dorje's conviction that the infant was the new Karmapa incarnation, prompted the eighth Shamar Rinpoche to send a search party to find and test the boy. The party was conducted to the house by Terton Minjur Dorje himself. Changchub Dorje satisfied Shamarpa's representatives that he was indeed the Karmapa incarnation. Subsequently, he was named Changchub Dorje by Shamar Rinpoche. During his early years he was instructed by several noted meditation masters and scholars, including Situ Chokyi Jungnay, Tsuglak Tenpi Nyingje and Nyenpa Tulku. At the age of seven, he arrived at Karma Gon. A little later Changchub Dorje journeyed to Kampo Gangra where he did some intensive meditation. From there he traveled to the Nangchen principality.

On the way to Tsurphu, the young Karmapa made a pilgrimage to the caves at Baram, where Baram Darma Wangchuk had been in retreat. Barampa had been a close disciple of Gampopa and had founded the Baram Kagyu lineage.

Finally, Changchub Dorje's party reached Tsurphu, where he continued his studies. Karmapa's innate spirituality unfolded itself in his dreams. He had a natural affinity for the teachings of the *Kālacakra Tantra* and in one night he dreamt that he visited Śambhala, where he received the empowerment and textual transmission of Kālacakra from King Rigden of Śambhala, who was the holder of the Kālacakra teaching lineage.

The lifetime of the twelfth Karmapa was again a troubled period. The Dzungarian Mongols attacked central Tibet, killing Lapzang Khan, Minling Lotsawa Dharma Śrī, Padma Gyurme Gyatsho and many other great Nyingma masters. During four years of conflict, many monasteries were destroyed, including Mindroling and Dorje Drag. Relics and treasures were stolen and the entrances to the Padmasambhava caves were obstructed.

When the seventh Dalai Lama, Kalzang Gyatsho returned from Kham, the invaders retreated. Changchub Dorje went to visit Kalzang Gyatsho to whom he made appropriate offerings and received the latter's blessing.

When Karmapa had arrived back at Tsurphu he was visited by Katok Tsewang Norbu, to whom he gave teachings on the six *yogas* of Nāropa and *mahāmudrā*. This *lama* was a famed meditation master and *terton* of the Katok Nyingma lineage. He in turn instructed Changchub Dorje in some Nyingma doctrine.

Karmapa set out on a pilgrimage to the sacred places of Nepal. Included in his party were Shamar Rinpoche, Situ Rinpoche and the seventh Gyaltshap Rinpoche. They were welcomed in Kathmandu by King Jagajayamalla, who feted them with a great ceremony. During his stay in Nepal, Changchub Dorje visited Yanglayshod, where Guru Padmasambhava accomplished the meditation on Vajrakīlaya in order to destroy all hindrances to his compassionate activity. There, Karmapa and his party performed spiritual practices of Padmasambhava in wrathful aspect, and thus, renewed the link with the inspiration of the "Lotus Born" guru.

An influenza epidemic had broken out in the Kathmandu valley and Changchub Dorje's aid was required. Karmapa performed the spiritual practice of Avalokiteśvara first, and then having symbolically purified an amount of water with the compassion of Avalokiteśvara, he, together with the other *lamas* in his party, blessed the area in a water purification ceremony. The epidemic was stopped and the king arranged a festive celebration in Karmapa's honor.

Subsequently, Changchub Dorje, together with Shamarpa and Situ Rinpoche, traveled on to Kuśinagara in northern India, the place of

Śākyamuni Buddha's decease. Throughout the journey, Situ Rinpoche's sophisticated scholarship greatly impressed the Hindu *paṇḍitas* whom he met in discussion. Many became his students as a result of his mastery of philosophy and linguistics.

On the return journey to Tibet, Karmapa and his party visited a cave in the vicinity of Jomo Gangkar mountain, where Lesom Gendun Bum, Milarepa's principal female student, had practiced intensive meditation. The party then visited Mount Kailāsa, which was renowned as the spiritual environment of Cakrasaṃvara. About this time Changchub Dorje received an invitation to visit China from the emperor, Yung Ching. He decided to accept the invitation and together with Shamarpa, Situpa and Gyaltshabpa, he slowly traveled back to Tsurphu.

Having arrived back at Tsurphu, Karmapa did not set out immediately for China. He went into retreat and then visited Lhasa and traveled to southern Tibet, giving teachings to many people. Changchub Dorje met Surmang Trungpa Rinpoche, on whom he bestowed the *mahāmudrā* and the six *yogas* of Nāropa.

Karmapa entrusted Situ Chokyi Jungnay with the guardianship of the Karma Kagyu school, during his visit to China. In addition, Situ Rinpoche was asked to complete all the texts that Karmapa and Shamarpa had started. In 1725, after giving Situpa some empowerments, Changchub Dorje and Shamar Rinpoche set out for China. When the party reached Amdo province, Karmapa performed a special ceremony for world peace. Later Changchub Dorje performed another ceremony at Lake Kokonor.

As he traveled on into China, Karmapa gave teachings and empowerments, especially that of Vajrapāṇi, embodiment of the power of buddhahood. Changchub Dorje met with the rulers of the districts through which he passed and discussed *dharma* with them. The party finally arrived at Lan Chu in 1732, where Changchub Dorje visited the Tārā and Avalokiteśvara temples, as well as the Taoist temples. While in Lan Chu, Karmapa contracted smallpox. He sent a letter containing details of his next rebirth to Situ Rinpoche. On the thirtieth day of the tenth month of the year of the Water Rat (1732) he passed away.

The principal students of Changchub Dorje were Situ Chokyi Jungnay, Pawo Tsuglak Dondrup and his reincarnation, Drukchen Kagyu Thinley Zhingta.

13
Karmapa Dudul Dorje
(1733–1797)

THE THIRTEENTH KARMAPA, Dudul Dorje, was born in Chaba Drong, a village four days journey from Lhasa, in the eighth month of the year of the Water Ox (1733 C.E.). Shortly after this, Lama Katok Tsewang Norbu had a vision, in which he saw the exact birthplace of Karmapa.

The infant had a birthmark on his tongue in the shape of the Tibetan letter *a,* and as he grew, he displayed remarkable natural spirituality. The young Karmapa was said to be able to recall events from his past lives. On one early occasion Dudul Dorje had a highly significant vision of the *dharma* protector, the Vajra Black-Cloaked One, in the form of a young boy dressed in a white silk robe and holding a crystal plate full of flowers. Dudul Dorje asked the apparition, "Who are you?" Immediately the *dharma* protector assumed his completely overwhelming wrathful form and declared, "I am the glorious roaring Vajra Black-Cloaked One. I arise in wrathful form from the space of transcendent wisdom. I perform the four activities of pacifying, enriching, integrating and destroying.[1] This is the ultimate view." In this way the *dharma* protector symbolically pointed to the *mahāmudrā* teaching that there is nothing separate from mind. Then the vision disappeared into space. The power of this experience was so strong that it communicated itself to everyone around Dudul Dorje.

By the time he reached the age of four the young boy's fame had spread far and wide. Gyaltshap Rinpoche sent a search party who located the child, who was then taken to Tsurphu, where Gyaltshabpa officially recognized and enthroned him as the thirteenth Karmapa. In this elaborate ceremony Dudul Dorje received his black crown. The seventh Dalai Lama, Kalzang Gyatsho, and his prime minister, Pholha Sonam Thobjay, sent their greetings to the new Karmapa.

A little while after his enthronement, Dudul Dorje was visited in Tsurphu by the most scholarly eighth Situ, Chokyi Jungnay. Situpa was delighted to see the incarnation of Changchub Dorje, his own spiritual father, and gave the young boy a comprehensive range of Karma Kagyu teachings. At the age of fourteen, Dudul Dorje was ordained a novice by Situ Rinpoche in Tsurphu. The ceremony took place before the famous statue of the Buddha constructed by Karma Pakshi.

The thirteenth Karmapa's education continued after his ordination and mainly followed the Kagyu and Nyingma traditions. He received the empowerments of the *Kālacakra Tantra* together with its associated teachings. His studies and practice also included the teachings of Dusum Khyenpa and the teachings of the six volumes composed by Rigdzin Jatson Nyingpo, the famous Nyingma *terton* and student of the tenth Karmapa, who introduced the Konchog Chidu[2] cycle. In addition, Dudul Dorje mastered the *Hevajra Tantra*, the *Ocean of Ḍākinīs* (Tib.: *ṁkha.'gro.rgya. mtsho*), Madhyamaka philosophy, *abhidharma*, *vinaya*, and the *sūtras*. In this fashion he received the most important streams of spiritual practice current in his day.

At the age of thirty-one, the thirteenth Karmapa was ordained a monk by Situ Rinpoche. Subsequently, he perfected his practice of the six *yogas* of Nāropa and *mahāmudrā* and received the complete transmission of the lineage from Situ Rinpoche. Dudul Dorje blended together the two lifestyles of scholar and "crazy-wisdom" yogin, and he embodied the compassionate spontaneity of awakened energy. His love for animals became legendary. It is said that he communicated the essence of *dharma* to birds, mice, cats, rabbits and bees. Each day he spent much time with the creatures, who flocked to him, as well as with his human students.

Dudul Dorje was himself the subject of one of Padmasambhava's prophecies. At one time Lhasa was threatened by the flooding waters of the Tsangpo or Chichu, Happy River, or as it is known in India, the Brahmaputra River. It was recalled that in a book of prophecy by Guru Padma, it was said that if Lhasa was ever in danger of being flooded, Karmapa's blessing should be requested. In accordance with this, the capital's authorities asked him to come as quickly as possible. Dudul Dorje arrived in Lhasa and averted the danger by invoking the inspiration of Avalokiteśvara and Śākyamuni.

In 1772 Karmapa traveled to Dege to see the aged Situ Rinpoche. Dudul Dorje journeyed through Kham, teaching and bestowing his blessing. He met with the tenth Shamar Rinpoche, Mipham Chodrup Gyatsho.[3] At Danang in Kham, Karmapa performed a special ceremony for Karma monastery. The ceremony was sponsored by the Danang noble family, who presented Dudul Dorje with a gold and silver vase. During his stay, Karmapa remarked to the family that he would return to them in the future, saying "Soon we shall meet again. When it happens you will understand it in detail. Keep this in mind."

Dudul Dorje lived in a very simple fashion and distributed his wealth both to the needy and to religious projects. He financed the construction of many *dharma* centers and also the printing of texts.

In his later years a famous demonstration of apparently miraculous energy of the Karmapa took place. Messengers from Powo Gyaldzong in southeastern Tibet arrived at Tsurphu and invited Karmapa to bless their monastery. Dudul Dorje was unable to go but on the appointed day he gave the blessing while still in Tsurphu. Simultaneously, the assembled crowds at Powo Gyaldzong witnessed a rain of blessed barley from the sky.

In 1774 Karmapa had a vision indicating the location of the new Situ incarnation. He sent a party to the place indicated, where they found the infant. Subsequently, Dudul Dorje officially recognized and enthroned the new Situ, Padma Nyingche Wangpo.

In 1797, at the age of sixty-four, having entrusted his incarnation letter to Situ Rinpoche, Dudul Dorje passed away. His remains were enshrined in a one story high silver *stūpa* in Tsurphu. His monks also made a silver statue of Karmapa.

Among the thirteenth Karmapa's principal students were Situ Padma Nyingche Wangpo, the Drukchen Kunzig Chokyi Nangwa, Pawo Tsuglak Chogyal, the Ladakhi prince, Hemi Gyalsay, Khamtrul Jigme Senge, and Sangye Nyenpa Tulku.

14

Karmapa Thegchog Dorje

(1798–1868)

THE FOURTEENTH KARMAPA, Thegchog Dorje, was born in Salmo Gang in Kham, the village of the Danang family, in the year of the Fire Snake (1798 C.E.). During her pregnancy, his mother had had several auspicious dreams, indicating the birth of an incarnate *guru*. It is recorded that, on the day of his birth, rainbows appeared and flowers bloomed, even though it was in the depths of the winter. The newborn child was heard to recite the Sanskrit alphabet.

News of the prodigy traveled quickly and a search party was dispatched by Drukchen Chokyi Nangwa to find the incarnation of his *guru*. This party, having reached Salmo Gang, met with two other parties from Situ Rinpoche and Gyaltshap Rinpoche. Together they conducted the child to Ogmin monastery, where they determined that the details of his birth matched exactly those set out in the previous Karmapa's letter of prediction. The ninth Situ, Padma Nyinche Wangpo, formally recognized Thegchog Dorje as the new Karmapa. He also ordained him as a novice. For the next few years at Ogmin Ling, Thegchog Dorje studied the doctrines of the Kagyu and Nyingma traditions.

After being enthroned and receiving the *vajra* crown, the fourteenth Karmapa went to Tsurphu, where he continued his studies. At the age of nineteen he was ordained a monk by Situ Rinpoche and Drukchen Chokyi Nangwa. During this period he engaged in the rebuilding and repair of the monastery itself and many of the *stūpas* and temples in the surrounding area. Thegchog Dorje was himself highly expert in various arts and crafts, including sculpture and metal work.

The fourteenth Karmapa was an accomplished scholar and linguist. He devoted much of his time to poetry and was especially skilled in rhetoric and poetics. During his lifetime there occurred the great Buddhist renaissance in Tibet, due largely to the Rime movement. This movement, which originated in Kham, was led by many teachers from the various traditions such as Jamgon Kongtrul Lodro Thaye, Khyentse Wangpo and Terton Chogyur Lingpa. It was not an attempt to form a new school or organization, but rather it sought to bring together and make available the richness of each tradition to everybody. Those involved in the movement were not just religious scholars and meditators, but were also talented artists, poets, doctors and even scientists, as was Mipham Rinpoche.

Thegchog Dorje both influenced and was himself influenced by this trend. He gave lineage teachings to Jamgon Kongtrul and Jamyang Khyentse Wangpo as well as certain specific teachings to the former. From the great *terton,* Chogyur Lingpa, he received the great *sādhana* of Vajrakīlaya. Subsequently he instituted the yearly performance of this ritual, alternating with the *tsechu* dance ritual of Padmasambhava, at Tsurphu.

The fourteenth Karmapa was renowned for his personal austerity and his strictness as a monk. Although he was himself the embodiment of compassion, Thegchog Dorje demanded complete observance of the monastic rules from those around him.

In the 1860s Karmapa traveled throughout Kham, working continually for the the benefit of the people. He recognized and enthroned the tenth Situ, Padma Kunzang, at Palpung monastery. During his stay there he gave teachings to Kongtrul Lodro Thaye, the profound Rime scholar. After his guru had returned to Tsurphu, Kongtrul Lodro Thaye followed to continue studying with him. Shortly before Karmapa's death Lodro Thaye received the transmission of the lineage from him.

Thegchog Dorje passed away in 1868 at the age of seventy. His principal students were Kongtrul Lodro Thaye, Drukchen Mipham Chokyi Gyatsho, Dechen Chogyur Lingpa, Pawo Tsuglak Nyingche and Jamyang Khyentse Wangpo.

15

Karmapa Khakhyab Dorje

(1871–1922)

THE FIFTEENTH KARMAPA, Khakhyab Dorje, was born in Shelkar in Tsang province in the year of the Iron Sheep (1871 C.E.). The infant was marked by a tiny tuft of white hair that grew between his eyebrows, just as a similar tuft is said to have distinguished the body of the baby Śākyamuni. Khakhyab Dorje displayed remarkable intelligence at a tender age and by the time he was four, he was composing prayers.

At the age of six the child was recognized as the new Karmapa incarnation, in accordance with the details contained in the letter of prediction left by the fourteenth Karmapa. He was officially recognized by Kongtrul Lodro Thaye, Jamyang Khyentse and Drukchen Minjur Wangkyi Gyalpo and was crowned in the "golden throne ceremony" at Tsurphu. He was also ordained as a novice by Drukchen Rinpoche.

Khakhyab Dorje was an assiduous student. Even when very young he was taught basic *mahāyāna dharma,* logic and astrology. At the age of eight he constructed a Mahākāla shrine and also composed a prayer to the *dharmapāla.*

In 1881 Karmapa and his entourage paid a visit to the thirteenth Dalai Lama, Thubten Gyatsho and his court. On his return to Tsurphu he began to study with the very scholarly abbot of Palpung monastery, Khanchen Tashi Ozer, from whom he received the textual transmission of the entire *Tripiṭaka.* He also studied with the ninth Pawo Rinpoche, who instructed him in the six volumes of Rigdzin Jatson Nyingpo's *terma* (Tib.: *gter.chos*).

In 1886, Khakhyab Dorje went to see Kongtrul Rinpoche in Palpung monastery. The aged scholar gave Karmapa the empowerments, textual transmissions and instructions of his own *Five Treasures* (Tib.: *mdzod. lnga*). This series contains over one hundred volumes compiled, annotated and commented upon by Kongtrul Lodro Thaye. It presents the major and minor traditions of religious thought and practice from the Rime perspective and had had a profound influence upon the subsequent development of *dharma.* Kongtrul Rinpoche also gave Khakhyab Dorje the *bodhisattva* vows and the empowerments and teaching of Kālacakra.

From Palpung, Karmapa and his party traveled on to Dzongsar, a great Sakya monastery, where he received teachings from Jamyang Khyentse Rinpoche. At that time memories of his past lives were reawakened in Khakhyab Dorje and he composed poetry concerning the training of a *bodhisattva.* Somewhat later, Karmapa visited the famous head of the Drukpa Kagyu monastery of Sang Ngag Choling. He recognized the new Drukchen incarnation and gave him the five precepts.

In 1888, Khakhyab Dorje returned to study with Kongtrul Rinpoche. The contents of his studies ranged over Sanskrit, astrology, medicine, art, Madhyamaka, *Prajñāpāramitā, vinaya, abhidharma* and the *Five Dharmas of Maitreya.* Subsequently, Karmapa revisited Dzongsar monastery, where he received the empowerments of the *Collected Sādhanas* (Tib.: *sgrub.thab.kun.'dus*) of the Sakya tradition from Khyentse Rinpoche. After his return to Palpung, Kongtrul Rinpoche bestowed on him the teachings of the Shangpa Kagyu tradition. Throughout this period Khakhyab Dorje studied throughout the day and into the night.

In 1890 Karmapa recognized and enthroned the eleventh Situ Rinpoche, Padma Wangchuk Gyalpo. He also revisited Sang Ngag Choling, Lhasa and Samye as well as the pilgrimage place of Tsari where he discovered some *termas* and was protected by *ḍākas* and *ḍākinīs.*

On his arrival back at Tsurphu, Khakhyab Dorje established a new seminary and repaired the main shrine. He also constructed a new temple in Lhasa for the "five sisters of long life" (Tib.: *tshe.ring.mched.lnga*).[1] It was dedicated to the peace and happiness of Tibet and the rest of the world at the request of the Dalai Lama.

A little later, Karmapa returned to his guru, Kongtrul Rinpoche, at Palpung monastery and received the empowerments, teachings and textual transmissions of the Lama Gongdu cycle. Returning to Tsurphu, Khakhyab Dorje designed new ornaments and costumes for the ritual dances of the *dharmapāla,* Vajra Black-Cloaked One. He also commissioned Kongtrul Rinpoche's sixty-three volume *Precious Treasury* (Tib.: *rin.chen.gter.mdzod*) and his own works, the only complete collections of the works of Kagyu scholars to come out of Tibet.

In 1898 Khakhyab Dorje paid a brief visit to Bhutan on the invitation of the king, Urgyen Wangchuk. Karmapa was extensively honored and he gave the king instructions in *dharma* teachings.

On his return to Tibet, Khakhyab Dorje took several consorts in fulfillment of his guru's prediction. A little later he recognized the new incarnations of Kongtrul Rinpoche, his own son, and Pawo Rinpoche. He instructed them and Situ Rinpoche in Kagyu *dharma.* He transmitted the Kagyu lineage to Situpa, Kongtrul Rinpoche and Palpung Khyentse Rinpoche and then went into retreat for ten years.

In his fifty-first year, in 1922, Karmapa Khakhyab Dorje passed away. Several years earlier he had entrusted the details of his next incarnation to Jampal Tsultim, his favorite attendant. Ten years earlier, in 1912, he had also insisted that the new year trumpets be blown toward the east instead of the south as was customary.

Khakhyab Dorje's principal students were Situ Padma Wangchuk Gyalpo, Jamgon Kongtrul Khyentse Ozer, Palpung Khyentse Tulku, and Gyaltshap Rinpoche.

16

Karmapa Rangjung Rigpe Dorje

(1923–)

THE SIXTEENTH KARMAPA, Rangjung Rigpe Dorje, was born at Denkhok in the Dege region of Kham near the river Yangtse, on the full moon day of the sixth month of the year of the Wood Mouse (1923 C.E.). He was born into an aristocratic family named Athub. His father's name was Tsewang Norbu and his mother's Kalzang Choden. The birth of a great *bodhisattva* in the Athub family had been previously predicted by Dzok Chen Tulku, Chokyi Dorje, head of the famous Nyingma monastery of Dzok Chen. Acting on his advice, the mother had given birth in the nearby cave of Padmasambhava, called the Lion Sky Castle.

Before the child's birth he disappeared entirely from the womb for one whole day and then returned the next. On the actual night of his birth, the atmosphere was charged with portents, which everyone in the locality could sense.

Shortly afterwards, Situ Padma Wangchuk Gyalpo opened the previous Karmapa's letter of prediction and discovered therein a detailed description of the house in which Rangjung Rigpe Dorje's parents dwelt. A search party was sent, and the child was speedily recognized to be the sixteenth Karmapa incarnation.

When he was seven years old he received the novice ordination from Situ Rinpoche and Jamgon Kongtrul of Palpung. A year later the *vajra* crown and the robes of the Karmapa were brought from Tsurphu to Kham for him. Situ Rinpoche then invited him to visit Palpung monastery.

On the way there, Karmapa's party was met by the prince of Dege, Tsewang Dudul, who requested Karmapa to visit his palace. This palace, Dege Lhundrup Teng, which was built by the fifteenth century Nyingma saint, Thangtong Gyalpo, was near Dege Gonchen, the main monastery of the Sakya Ngorpa lineage. While in Dege, Rangjung Rigpe Dorje visited and blessed the monastery's huge printing press. A little later the party traveled on to Palpung, where the young Karmapa was given a great welcome. Four days later he was enthroned by Situ Rinpoche in the main shrine of the monastery.

On the twenty-third day of the fourth month of the Iron Sheep year, Rangjung Rigpe Dorje and Situ Rinpoche, accompanied by a monastic camp of a thousand people called Karmapa *garchen,* set out for Tsurphu. Along the way, Rangjung Rigpe Dorje performed the *vajra* crown ceremony for the first time in his lifetime at Gyina Gompa in Nangchen. After this auspicious event, the party visited Nyenchen Thanglha, an environment symbolically dedicated to the energy of the Karma Kagyu tradition. On his subsequent arrival at Tsurphu, Karmapa was welcomed by Palpung Kongtrul Rinpoche, Pawo Rinpoche and Gyaltshap Rinpoche.

After a short period of time Rangjung Rigpe Dorje visited the thirteenth Dalai Lama in Lhasa, from whom he received the "hair cutting" ceremony. During this ceremony, the Dalai Lama, Thubten Gyatsho, perceived the *vajra* crown, woven from the hair of one hundred thousand *ḍākinīs,* above the head of Rangjung Rigpe Dorje. After his return to Tsurphu, Karmapa was given a second "golden throne ceremony" by Situ Rinpoche and Drukchen Rinpoche, Mipham Chokyi Wangpo, head of the Drukpa Kagyu sect.

For the next four years Rangjung Rigpe Dorje studied with Beru Khyentse Rinpoche and Bo Kangkar Mahāpaṇḍita, who was acclaimed as the last great Kaṃtshang Kagyu scholar of the time. Kangkar Rinpoche had memorized the entire contents of the *Tripiṭaka* and numbered among his students the profound contemporary Sakya scholar, Dezhung Rinpoche, as well as the eminent translator, Garma C. C. Chang. While studying with Kangkar Rinpoche, Karmapa related the stories of his previous lives to his guru.

In 1937 Rangjung Rigpe Dorje and his entourage set out on a journey to Dege in Kham, to visit Situ Rinpoche. On the journey many highly symbolic events took place which conveyed the inspiration of Karmapa's energy. Karmapa was invited to visit the king of Nangchen's palace and Tsechu Gompa, the Drukpa Kagyu monastery under the patronage of the king. He also visited Kaycha Gompa, a Drukpa Kagyu convent in Nangchen housing nine hundred nuns, the largest convent in Tibet.

In the area of Drong Tup there is a small lake in which it is said that Rangjung Rigpe Dorje left footprints in the water, which may be seen by anyone, even in winter when the lake is frozen. At Riwa Parma monastery as Karmapa performed the rituals of the wrathful Padmasambhava festival, fire flamed from the *tormas* ("offering cakes").

A little later Karmapa visited the monastery of the nineteenth century master, Chogyur Lingpa, the last great *terton.* There Lama Samten Gyatsho requested Karmapa to bring an end to the drought that was afflicting the monastery. In response, Rangjung Rigpe Dorje asked for some water in which to wash himself. As he bathed it started to rain and a spring came up under the washtub.

When Karmapa finally arrived at Palpung monastery he was welcomed by Situ Rinpoche. Subsequently, Situpa instructed his student in Kongtrul Lodro Thaye's profound works, the *Kagyu Ngagdzod,* which contains the advanced *tantric* teachings of Marpa Lotsawa, and the *Dam Ngagdzod,* containing the advanced teachings of the eight original Tibetan Buddhist sects. On a visit to Pangphug monastery, Karmapa and Situ Rinpoche left their footprints in stone. While outside the temple, Rigpe Dorje's dog and horse also left clear footprints in the rock.

After a short meditation retreat, Karmapa and Situ Rinpoche received an invitation to visit China from General Chang Kai Shek. However, Karmapa did not accept the invitation personally, choosing instead to send Beru Khyentse Rinpoche as his representative.

At the Dzongsar monastery of Khyentse Chokyi Lodro, the great Rime scholar, Rigpe Dorje performed the *vajra* crown ceremony. Khyentse Rinpoche envisaged the spiritual form of the *vajra* crown floating about eighteen inches above Karmapa's head. In addition, he saw Karmapa in the form of Dusum Khyenpa. On his return to Palpung, Rigpe Dorje received the empowerments, textual transmissions and instructions of the collected spiritual practices of the Sakya tradition (Tib.: *sgrub.thabs.kun.btus*).

In the ninth month of the year of the Iron Dragon (1940), Karmapa began the journey back to Tsurphu. On the way, he visited Benchen monastery, where, on his arrival, a statue of the horse on which the *dharmapāla* Zhingchong (Tib.: *zhing.skyong.*) was seated began to neigh. After a journey lasting eleven months, Rigpe Dorje and his entourage reached Tsurphu. For the next three years, Karmapa entered into intensive practice, while new construction work was carried out on the monastery. In 1944 he went on a pilgrimage, first to Samye monastery and then on to Lhodrak, the home of Marpa Lotsawa. That same year Rigpe Dorje was invited to visit Bhutan at the request of the second king, Jigme Wangchuk.

During his stay he performed the *vajra* crown ceremony several times and gave many empowerments.

In the following year the aged Situ Rinpoche traveled to Tsurphu to give further teachings to his spiritual son. The twenty-two year old Rigpe Dorje received full ordination as a monk from Situpa. In addition, his guru instructed him in the *Gyachen Kadzod* collection of Kongtrul Lodro Thaye and the *Chigshe Kundrol.* From Urgen Rinpoche, Karmapa received the complete empowerments and textual transmissions of Terton Chogyur Lingpa's teaching.

In the fourth month of the year of the Fire Pig (1947) Karmapa journeyed to western Tibet and from there on to India and Sikkim. In Nepal he performed the *vajra* crown ceremony and gave his blessings to the people. Rigpe Dorje then traveled to Lumbinī, the birthplace of Śākamuni Buddha. He also visited Vārāṇasī, the site of Śākyamuni's first sermon and Bodhgayā, the place of his enlightenment. At the invitation of the *mahārāja* of Sikkim, Tashi Namgyal, Karmapa visited Gangtok, where he performed the black crown ceremony and gave empowerments.

Rigpe Dorje then traveled to Rewalsar (Tib.: *mtsho.pad.ma*) in India, which is sacred to Padmasambhava. Many white snakes appeared on the surface of the lake there and this was regarded as a very auspicious event. During the long journey back to Tsurphu he passed through the area of Mount Kailāsa and Lake Manasarowar. Finally Karmapa and his party arrived back in Tsurphu in the eleventh month of the year of the Earth Rat (1948).

Rigpe Dorje invited Jamgon Kongtrul of Palpung to come to Tsurphu and give him further teachings. Kongtrul Rinpoche gave him the *Rinchen Terdzod,* and, in addition, instructions in *mahāmudrā* and the six *yogas* of Nāropa. At the completion of his studies, Rigpe Dorje received the textual transmission of the lineage from Kongtrul Rinpoche and Situ Rinpoche. To celebrate Karmapa's mastery of *mahāmudrā,* Palpung Kongtrul composed a poem in which he praised him as being a perfect holder of the *mahāmudrā* lineage. During this period an outbreak of smallpox reached epidemic proportions but was brought under control as a result of a Vajrakīlaya exorcism performed by Karmapa.

In the early years of the 1950s Karmapa carried on his teaching and administrative duties both in Tsurphu and in other parts of the country. In 1953, Rigpe Dorje gave the empowerments and textual transmissions of Dechen Chogyur Lingpa's *terma* teaching to Mindrol Ling Chong Rinpoche, who as head of the Mindrol Ling monastery was in effect the senior *lama* of the Nyingma tradition.

In 1954 the Chinese authorities in Peking invited His Holiness the fourteenth Dalai Lama, and the heads of the other Tibetan religious traditions, together with other dignitaries, to visit Peking and other parts of China. His Holiness Karmapa accepted the invitation and, together with the rest of the party, traveled to Peking. While there, Karmapa received a visionary intimation from Mahākāla indicating the circumstances of the rebirth of Situ Rinpoche. He was able to send a letter to Palpung describing the whereabouts of the Situ incarnation. On the return journey, Karmapa formally enthroned the new Situpa at Palpung. He also traveled extensively throughout Kham as the personal ambassador of the Dalai Lama in an attempt to restore calm to an increasingly worried populace. Many Kagyu *lamas* and students came to Karmapa while he traveled, to receive empowerments and ordinations.

Following his return to Tsurphu, Karmapa supervised the construction of a residence for His Holiness the Dalai Lama, whom he invited to visit. The Dalai Lama and his entourage were greeted with great festivities and he was requested to give the empowerment of the one thousand armed Avalokiteśvara. In return the Dalai Lama asked Karmapa to perform the ceremony of the *vajra* crown. During the visit Rigpe Dorje showed the Dalai Lama the wealth of relics collected at Tsurphu and a ritual Padmasambhava dance was held in his honor.

In the same year, 1955, serious hostilities broke out in the Dege and Nangchen districts of Kham. Karmapa visited Chamdo, where he tried to bring about peace between the Khampas and the Chinese forces. Both sides promised to keep a five year truce.

In 1956 His Holiness visited Druk Dechen Chokhor Ling, the principal Drukpa Kagyu monastery. He gave teachings and also performed a purification rite. From there he traveled on to Sikkim, where he again met the king, Tashi Namgyal. The year 1956 was celebrated worldwide as the twenty-five hundredth anniversary of Lord Buddha's *parinirvāṇa,* so Karmapa and his party extended their journey into India and Nepal, where they visited all the sacred places of pilgrimage. From Nepal, Rigpe Dorje returned to India and the famed Ajantā caves, which contain Buddhist carvings made during the Gupta dynastic period. In Kalimpong, Karmapa met with Her Royal Highness Azhi Wangmo, the Bhutanese princess, who undertook to build a monastery for His Holiness in eastern Bhutan. At this time, Rigpe Dorje was asked to visit Rumtek monastery in Sikkim, which had been established during the lifetime of the ninth Karmapa. However, he declined the invitation, saying that he would be coming to it in the future, when he had need of it.

When Rangjung Rigpe Dorje returned to Tsurphu early in 1957, serious hostilities had broken out again in Kham. A stream of refugees was pouring into central Tibet. Among these refugees were many Kagyu *lamas* such as the ninth Sangye Nyenpa Rinpoche, Situ Rinpoche, Talep Rinpoche and their followers who came to Tsurphu. During this time Karmapa recognized the twelfth Gyaltshap incarnation the new Palpung Kongtrul Rinpoche, and Bongsar Khyentse, Rinpoche. From Zechen Kongtrul, Karmapa himself received the textual transmissions and teachings of the *Longchen Dzodun,* the profound seven volume work of Longchenpa, which deals with *mahā ati.*

Inexorably, the conflict spread from Kham into central Tibet. Karmapa sent Situ Rinpoche, Sangye Nyenpa Rinpoche and the venerable meditation master, Kalu Rinpoche, to Bhutan. The young Palpung Jamgon Kongtrul was sent to Kalimpong in India to stay with his family, wealthy merchants, the Sandu. However, Karmapa himself decided not to leave at that time, saying that he would come to Bhutan if the situation deterioriated. It was his intention to stay behind in Tsurphu until the last possible moment in order to render assistance to the refugees.

The hostilities between the Chinese Communist army and the Khampa resistance were now raging throughout Tibet. From all appearances the ancient Buddhist culture of Tibet was about to be extinguished like the light of a lamp. Realizing that he must leave Tibet now, in order to help preserve *buddhadharma,* Rigpe Dorje informed the Dalai Lama of his plans. Subsequently, in the middle of the fourth night of the second month of the year of the Earth Pig (1959), Karmapa, dressed in lay clothing, together with a party of one hundred and sixty people, left Tsurphu, carrying some precious relics and shrine implements that were light in weight. The party included incarnate *lamas,* monks and lay people. With Karmapa were the thirteenth Shamar Rinpoche, the twelfth Gyaltshap Rinpoche, the meditation master, Drupon Tenzin Rinpoche, Dabtrul Rinpoche, Khandro Chenmo, the saintly fourth consort of Karmapa Khakhyab Dorje, and others including His Holiness's general secretary, Dorje Lopon Topga Rinpoche and the author.

The party's escape route lay over the Himalayas into Bhutan. However, the food supply was only sufficient for two weeks. Karmapa's party passed through southern Tibet and the local people gave much assistance to the refugees. Fleeting visits were paid along the way to Marpa Lotsawa's house in Lhodrak and also to a Milarepa shrine, the famous nine story tower built at Marpa Lotsawa's direction, where His Holiness gave the Milarepa initiation and performed the *sādhana.*

As the group reached the last snow pass, Mon La Gar Chung (elevation 19,855 ft.), which marks the Tibet-Bhutan border, Karmapa urged everyone on, saying that they must cross the pass that same day. The party expended their last energy in crossing over into Bhutan, assisted by guides from the local people. During the following night there was a great snowfall, which blocked all the passes for two or three days. In fact, the military forces had been in close pursuit of the refugees, and had they not done as Karmapa directed they would have been captured.

Twenty-one days after leaving Tsurphu, Karmapa and his party arrived in the Bumthang district of Bhutan, the land said to bear the footprints of one hundred thousand *ḍākinīs.* He was given a very warm welcome by the Bhutanese princess and nun, Azhi Wangmo, and others. Kalu Rinpoche, together with his monks, came to visit Karmapa in Tashi Chodzong, as did Situ Rinpoche. Having visited King Jigme Dorge Wangchuk in Thimphu, the Bhutanese capital, Karmapa decided to move on into India.

At Baxa, on the border of Bhutan and India, His Holiness met with the Sikkimese Prime Minister, Banya Sahib Tashi Dadul, who conveyed the *mahārāja's* invitation to Karmapa to reside in Sikkim. Karmapa decided to accept the invitation, and on the twenty-fifth day of the fourth month of the year of the Earth Pig (1959) he and his party went to Gangtok, the Sikkimese capital. Karmapa was warmly welcomed by the royal family and the people, and was asked where he would like to settle. He replied that as Tibetan refugees they hoped one day to be able to return to Tibet. Therefore, their residence would in one sense be only temporary. However, as the ninth Karmapa, Wangchuk Dorje had commissioned the building of Rumtek monastery, he, the sixteenth Karmapa, would like to establish his seat-in-exile there.

Following his arrival at Rumtek, Karmapa ceremonially enthroned Palpung Kongtrul Rinpoche and bestowed many empowerments upon him. That winter (1959–60), Rigpe Dorje visited India, where he first met

His Holiness the Dalai Lama in Benares and later Paṇḍit Nehru, the then prime minister, who was very sympathetic both to Buddhism and the plight of the Tibetan refugees. In the summer Karmapa gave many empowerments to large numbers of people who flocked to see him. Large sums of money were donated to Karmapa from the Sikkimese and Indian governments to aid in the construction of a new monastery, situated on seventy acres of land near the old Rumtek monastery. The site chosen had many auspicious signs: seven hills facing, seven streams flowing toward it, a mountain behind it, snow mountains in front of it, and a river below, twirling in the shape of a conch shell. The great enthusiasm for the work among Karmapa's followers meant that the construction was accomplished in four years.

During this period His Holiness recognized the new Drukchen Rinpoche, Drukpa Yongdzin Rinpoche, Dzigar Choktor Rinpoche, the two new Sangye Nyenpa *tulkus* (one of whom was born in America), Surmang Garwang Rinpoche, Drongram Jatrul, the new Dzok Chen Ponlob incarnation and Drupon *tulku* Chogyur Lingpa.

Up to the present time His Holiness Karmapa has ordained more than 3,000 monks and recognized hundreds of *tulkus*. He has caused to be published a new printing of the Dege *Kanjur*, the basic encyclopedia of Buddha's teaching. In a gesture of interdenominational cooperation and fellowship, he has distributed 170 sets to institutions of all four sects of Tibetan Buddhism and to representatives of the Bonpo faith. His Holiness has made two extended trips around the world. Several of his own Karma Kagyu *lamas* have established *dharma* centers in the West, and His Holiness has toured them and given teachings.

This has been a concise account of the lives of the sixteen Karmapas. For more detailed accounts one should consult the original records and biographies. However, in the final analysis all records are limited. The Karmapa's unborn nature, knowing past, present and future, perfectly realizing the teachings of *dharma*, and effortlessly radiating the liberating power of compassion, completely transcends the network of concepts.

NOTES

In order to keep this section brief, we have endeavored to cover the main points and details of Kagyu teaching in the section, The Historical and Theoretical Background. Many references in the text may therefore be clarified by referring to the introduction.

INTRODUCTION

1. Rudyard Kipling, "The Ballad of East and West" (1889), *The Collected Works of Rudyard Kipling* (AMS Press, 1941).

2. David Snellgrove, trans., in *Buddhist Texts through the Ages,* ed. Edward Conze (New York: Harper & Row, 1964), p. 233.

THE HISTORICAL AND THEORETICAL BACKGROUND

1. Words from the Tibetan and Sanskrit occur throughout the text. Wherever they have not been translated into English, they appear in an anglicized spelling. Many of these Sanskrit and Tibetan words are followed by transcriptions, within parentheses and preceded by "Skt." and "Tib." respectively, which indicate their exact spelling in the original languages. At the end of the text there is a glossary containing transcriptions of Tibetan personal and place names.

2. For further detail see *A Political History of Tibet* by Shakabpa, *Karmapa: The Black Hat Lama of Tibet* by Nik Douglas and Meryl White, and the *History of the Karma Kagyupa Sect* by Situ Panchen and Belo Tsewang Kunchab.

CHAPTER 1. DUSUM KHYENPA

1. *Vinaya* is the third of the three baskets *(Tripiṭaka)* enunciated by Śākyamuni Buddha. It is concerned with the discipline of the monastic community *(saṅgha)* and to a lesser extent with that of the lay community of *dharma* followers.

2. Virūpa was one of the most accomplished and influential of the eighty-four Buddhist *mahāsiddhas* of medieval India. Originally a monk and scholar at Vikramaśīla, the famous monastic university, he subsequently became a *tantric yogin.* Under the inspiration of Vajradhara he elaborated the "path and fruit" doctrine, which was later transmitted in Tibet within the Sakya tradition.

3. See the *Blue Annals* of 'Gos Lotsawa, Book VIII, page 476, translated by George Roerich. Many of the incidents related in the lives of the first six Karmapas are also alluded to in the *Blue Annals,* Book VIII, which contains an account of the lives of these Karmapas and the early Kagyu tradition.

4. "Beyond meditation" (Tib.: *bsgom.med*) is the fourth and final stage of *mahāmudrā* meditation wherein the *yogin* transcends the notions of meditation and attainment. At this level, the whole phenomenal world arises as the *mahāmudra.*

5. "Dream *yoga*" is a particular aspect of *anuttara tantra yoga* in which the practitioner extends meditative awareness through the understanding and transformation of dreams. Certain dream *yoga* practices are associated with various deities such as Amitābha and Tārā. Dream *yoga* is also one of the six doctrines of Nāropa.

6. Vajraghaṇṭā was one of the eighty-four *mahāsiddhas.* He was famed for his magical powers and is particularly associated with the Cakrasaṃvara cycle. The dates of his birth and death are 1126–1225 C.E.

7. Śākyaśrī (1145–1225) was an immensely learned Kashmiri *paṇḍita* who was invited to Tibet to establish a firm monastic ordination line. He became the principal guru of Sakya Paṇḍita Kunga Gyaltsen through whom his influence spread.

8. Indrabhūti was an eighth century *tantric yogin* famed as one of the eighty-four *mahāsiddhas.* He reigned as King of Uḍḍiyāṇa in the northwest of India and became the adoptive father of Padmasambhava. He is associated with the *anuttara tantra* tradition.

9. Princess Lakṣmīṅkarā was a very accomplished *yoginī* and sister of King Indrabhūti. She composed the *tantric* text, *Jñānasiddhi.* See Dr. R. Ray's biographical article in *Loka 2: A Journal from Naropa Institute* (New York: Anchor Press/Doubleday, 1976).

CHAPTER 2. KARMA PAKSHI

1. Avalokiteśvara is the *bodhisattva* embodiment of the compassion of buddhahood, and the spiritual "son" of Buddha Amitābha, to whose *padma* ("lotus") "family" he belongs.

2. The ten virtues (Tib.: *dge.ba.bcu.ba*) of basic morality for both lay and ordained Buddhists comprise three sections pertaining to body, speech and mind. In relation to the body the virtues are non-violence, not stealing and sexual morality. In relation to speech the virtues are being truthful, gentle, conciliatory and meaningful. In relation to mind they are noncovetousness, nonaggression and correctness of view.

CHAPTER 3. RANGJUNG DORJE

1. *The Five Texts of Maitreya* comprises the *Mahāyānasūtrālaṃkāra,* the *Uttaratantra,* the *Abhisamayālaṃkāra,* the *Dharmadharmatāvibhaṅga* and the *Madhyāntavibhaṅga.* They were composed by the third/fourth century master Asaṅga, under the inspiration (Tib.: *byin.rlabs*) of Maitreya.

2. *Abhidharma* is the second of the three baskets of *dharma* enunciated by the Buddha. *Abhidharma* or "further *dharma*" specifically deals with the enumeration and analysis of psychological states. In particular, the *abhidharma* analysis is developed together with the *hīnayāna* meditative discipline of tranquillity and insight.

3. Yamāntaka (Tib.: *shin.rje*) is an important deity in both the "old" and "new" *tantric* traditions. The clear and penetrating wisdom of Yamāntaka is the slayer of death.

4. The *Saṃpuṭika* is a commentary on the *Śrī-sampa anuttara tantra* composed in the medieval period. This cycle is included in Jamgon Kongtrul's *Kagyu Ngagdzod.*

5. "The peaceful and wrathful deities" comprise the *ati maṇḍala* of the awakened state. The forty-two peaceful deities embody the *śūnyatā* ("emptiness") of buddhahood and the wrathful deities embody the *prabhāsvara* ("luminosity") of buddhahood.

6. The *ṣaḍaṅga yoga* is a series of *anuttara tantra yoga* practices derived from the Kālacakra cycle.

7. The *Kanjur* (Tib.: *bka'.gyur*) and *Tanjur* (Tib.: *bstan.'gyur*) comprise the canon of Tibetan Mahāyāna Buddhism. The *Kanjur* contains the complete *sūtra* and *tantra* teachings of Buddha, while the *Tanjur* contains the authoritative commentaries by the foremost Buddhist masters of India. The *Kanjur* and *Tanjur* were collected by the great Buddhist scholar, Buton Rinchendrup (1290–1364).

8. Ngok Chodor and Meton Tsonpo were two of the "four pillars," or principal disciples of Marpa. Ngok Choku Dorje was the most talented scholar among Marpa's students and received the transmision of *tantric* commentarial teaching from his *guru.* Meton Tsonpo particularly specialized in the teaching of Hevajra.

9. Yagde or Yagde Panchen (Tib.: *gyag.sde.pan.chen*) (1299–1378) was a master of both *sūtra* and *tantra,* learned in the teachings of the major *dharma* traditions in Tibet at that time. He is said to have studied with one hundred and eight teachers. His own students were likewise numerous.

CHAPTER 4. ROLPE DORJE

1. The transcendent nature of buddhahood is reflected in five aspects or buddha "families" (Skt.: *kula*), each of which effects the transformation of a defilement (Skt.: *kleśa*) into its underlying wisdom. Each family has a buddha and his court of male and female *bodhisattvas.*

2. "The Prayer of Samantabhadra" is a very important "oral tradition" prayer of the Nyingma lineage. It contains essential instructions for transference to the complete awareness of Samantabhadra, the primordial buddha.

CHAPTER 5. DEZHIN SHEGPA

1. *Arhat* is the term for sainthood within the *hīnayāna* path. In Tibetan the word is translated Drachompa (Tib.: *dgra.bcom.pa*), "he who has slain the foe" of the defilements. Traditionally it is held that the dispensation of Śākyamuni Buddha is protected by sixteen *arhat* disciples.

2. The *garuḍa* is the celestial hawk of Indian mythology, which hatches from its egg fully developed. It symbolizes the buddha-nature. It destroys the five snakes of the defilements.

3. A *stūpa* is a concrete representation of the body, speech and mind of the Buddha, venerated as a repository of relics and blessings.

CHAPTER 6. THONGWA DONDEN

1. The five *tantras* are *Cakrasaṃvara, Mahāmāyā, Vajrabhairava, Guhyasamāja* and *Hevajra*. The six doctrines of Niguma (Tib.: *nigu. chos. drug*) correspond to the six doctrines of Nāropa, Niguma having been Nāropa's consort. The doctrines are *yogas* of the inner heat, dream, luminosity, transference, illusory body and *bardo*.

2. The *Duk Ngal Shijay* doctrine ("Pacification of Suffering") was elaborated by Phadampa Sangye. It has now ceased to exist as an independent lineage.

3. Ḍombhi Heruka was an important Indian *tantric yogin,* who held the lineage of the path and fruit teaching which he received from his *guru* Virūpa. He transmitted many teaching in the form of songs.

4. Kunchen Rongtonpa (1367–1449) was a very eminent Sakyapa master. He studied under Ngorchen Kunga Zangpo, who founded the Ngor subsect of the Sakya tradition. Rongton Sheja Kunrig composed many important philosophical treatises on the *Prajñāpāramitā*. He founded the monastery of Nālandā in Phenyul. His principal student was Gorampa Sonam Senge.

5. Śambhala is the mystic kingdom where the holders of the Kālacakra doctrine dwell. It is held to be situated to the north of Tibet. King Sucandra of Śambhala received the Kālacakra teaching from Buddha and entrusted it to his successors.

CHAPTER 7. CHODRAG GYATSHO

1. For details consult the *History of the Karma Kagyupa Sect* by Situ Panchen and Belo Tsewang Kunchab.

CHAPTER 8. MIKYO DORJE

1. The eight moral precepts are the five basic precepts of the lay followers: nonviolence, not taking what is not given, sexual morality, no false or harmful speech and no intoxication, plus three special precepts: avoiding soft and luxurious beds, eating at improper times and jewelry, singing and dancing.

2. Gyalwa Choyang was one of the twenty-five principal students of Guru Padmasambhava in the eighth century. Gyalwa Choyang was a minister at the court of King Trisong Detsun. He received the spiritual practice of the deity Hayagrīva from Guru Padma, and subsequently achieved complete realization.

3. These are the *Mūlamadhyamakakārikā, Śūnyatāsaptatikārikā, Yuktiṣaṣtikākārikā, Vigrahavyāvartanīkārikā, Vaidalyasūtra,* and *Vyavahārasiddhi.*

4. Ngok Lotsawa was one of the chief students of Atīśa. He worked with his *guru* on translation of the *Prajñāpāramitā* literature and played a particularly important role in the establishment of Madhyamaka philosophy in Tibet.

CHAPTER 9. WANGCHUK DORJE

1. The four *dharmas* of Gampopa were communicated as the essence of the spiritual path by Gampopa. They are as follows: "Bless me that my mind may enter

the *dharma* / Bless me that *dharma* may follow the path / Bless me that the path may clarify confusion / Bless me that confusion may be transformed into wisdom."

CHAPTER 10. CHOYING DORJE

1. The *mantra* of the "perfection of wisdom" is *oṃ gate gate pāragate pārasaṃgate bodhi svāhā.* This *mantra* is the essence of the "perfection of wisdom" teaching, and is referred to in the *Heart Sūtra* as the pacifier of sufferings.

2. *Termas* are "treasure texts" which are concealed and later discovered by "treasure discoverers" (Tib.: *gter.ston*). Many treasures were buried by Guru Padmasambhava and his close disciples and were discovered by emanations of the *guru* in subsequent centuries. These are known as "earth treasures" (Tib.: *sa.gter*). "Thought *termas*" (Tib.: *dgong.gter*) are concealed in the vast expanse of awareness, and discovered in meditation by visionaries.

CHAPTER 11. YESHE DORJE

1. Lay ordination consists of taking refuge in the three jeweis and committing oneself to the five basic precepts (see note 1 to chapter 5), upon which the practitioner becomes a lay follower (Skt.: *upāsaka, upāsikā*).

CHAPTER 13. DUDUL DORJE

1. The four activities (Tib.: *phrin.las.bzhi*): pacifying, enriching, integrating and destroying, embody the energetic compassion of the awakened state. The *dharmapālas* are endowed with the four activities, with which they protect the energy of *dharma.*

2. Konchog Chidu (Tib.: *dkon.mchog,spyi.'dus*) is a famous *terma* cycle discovered by the sixteenth century master Rigdzin Jatson Nyingpo, an emanation of Guru Padmasambhava. This cycle has continued to exert a great influence on both the Nyingma and Kagyu traditions to this day.

3. A certain amount of controversy attends the history of the tenth Shamar Rinpoche. Among several disputed contentions, it is often stated that the tenth Shamar Rinpoche poisoned himself. However, a respected Nyingma scholar, contemporary with the tenth Shamarpa, makes special reference to his life in order to clear up misconceptions that were beginning to proliferate even at that time. In his collected works (Vol. 1, p. 201) Katok Tsewang Norbu relates that people were spreading false rumors about the tenth Shamar Rinpoche, who was a very great *lama.* Tsewang Norbu relates that in the Iron Dog year the Shamarpa was poisoned and that as a result his health declined considerably, however, he did not pass away until a couple of years later on the full moon day of the sixth month of the Water Mouse year at the age of fifty-one. After he passed away his personal property was taken by the Chinese and Nepalese.

CHAPTER 15. KHAKHYAB DORJE

1. The "five sisters of long life" are *ḍākinīs,* i.e., embodiments of feminine energy. The leader of the five is Tashi Tseringma, who was the mystic consort of Milarepa. The other four sisters are Thingi Zhalzongma (*mthing.gi.zhal.bzang.*

ma), Miyo Lobzangma (*mi.g.yo.blo.bzang.ma*), Chopan Drinzangma (*cod-.pan.mgrin.bzang.ma*) and Tadkar Drozangma (*gtad.dkar.'gro.bzang.ma*). They were put under obligation to protect the *dharma* by both Guru Padmasambhava and Milarepa. A Himalayan legend has it that Miyo Lobzangma resides somewhere on the slopes of Jomo Lungma (the local name for the mountain also known as Mount Everest, in the west, and Jomo Gangkar in the literature of Tibet).

GLOSSARY

A

Amdo	a.mdo
Athub	ah.thub
Azhi	a.zhi

B

Baram	'ba'.ram
Bardo	bar.do
Bare	ba.re
Benchen	ben.chen
Bengar	ban.sgar
Beru	be.ru
Bum	bum
Bumthang	bum.thang
Buton	bu.ston

C

Chaba	cha.ba
Chaggya	phyag.rgya
Chagmed	chags.med
Chamdo	chab.mdo
Chang	chang
Changchub	byang.chub
Chen	chen
Chenmo	chen.mo
Chen-nga	spyan.mnga'
Chenpo	chen.po
Chichu	skyid.chu
Chidu	spyi.'dus
Chigshe	gcig.shes
Chilung	spyi.lung
Chimed	chi.med
Chod	gcod
Choden	chos.ldan
Chodor	chos.dor
Chodrag	chos.grags
Chodrup	chos.'grub
Chodzin	chos.'dzin
Chodzong	chos.rdzong
Chogyal	chos.rgyal
Chogyur	mchog.'gyur
Chokden	mchog.ldan
Chokhor	chos.'khor
Choktor	mchog.sprul
Chokyi	chos.kyi
Cholay	phyogs.las
Choling	chos.gling
Chong	skyong
Chophel	chos.'phel
Choyang	chos.yang
Choying	chos.dbyings
Chuwar	chu.bar

D

Dak	dwags
Dakpo	dwags.po
Dam	gdams
Damchu	dam.chu
Dampa	dam.pa
Danang	da.nang
Darma	dar.ma
Dechen	bde.chen
Dege	de.rge

Denkhok	den.khok
Densa	gdan.sa
Desheg	de.gshegs
Desi	de.srid
Detsun	de.btsun
Dezhin	de.bzhin
Dezhung	de.zhung
Dingo	dil.mgo
Do Kham	mdo.khams
Dolma	sgrol.ma
Dom	dom
Donden	don.ldan
Dondrup	don.'grub
Dorje	rdo.rje
Drag	brag
Drakpa	'grags.pa
Drelong	dre.long
Drepung	'bras.spungs
Drigung	'bri.gung
Drogmi	'brog.mi
Drogon	dro.gon
Dromtonpa	'brom.ston.pa
Drong	'brong
Dronma	sgron.ma
Dru	gru
Drub Zhi	gru.bzhi
Druk	'brugs
Drukchen	'brugs.chen
Drukpa	'brugs.pa
Drupa	gru.pa
Drupon	grub.dpon
Dudjom	bdud.'joms
Dudul	bdud.'dul
Duldzin	'dul.'dzin
Dusum	dus.gsum
Dzachu	dza.chu
Dzigar	'dzi.sgar
Dzodun	mdzod.bdun
Dzok	rdzogs
Dzongsar	rdzong.gsar

G

Ga	rga
Gaden	dga.'ldan
Gadri	ga.'dris
Gampo	sgam.po
Gampopa	sgam.po.pa
Gang	sgang
Gangkar	gangs.dkar
Gangra	gangs.ra
Gangri	gangs.ri
Gangtok	sgang.tog
Garchen	sgar.chen
Garwang	gar.dbang
Gelugpa	dge.lugs.pa
Gendun	dge.'dun
Geshe	dge.bshes
Gocha	go.cha
Golok	go.lok
Gompa	dgon.pa
Gomtsul	sgom.tshul
Gon	dgon
Gongchen	dgongs.chen
Gongdu	dgongs.'dus
Gorampa	go.ram.pa
Gungtang	gung.thang
Gushri	gu.shri
Gyachen	rgya.chen
Gyaldzong	rgyal.rdzong
Gyalpo	rgyal.po
Gyalsay	rgyal.sras
Gyaltsen	rgyal.mtshan
Gyaltshap	rgyal.tshab
Gysltshabpa	rgyal.tshab.pa
Gyalwa	rgyal.ba
Gyare	rgya.ras
Gyatsho	rgya.mtsho
Gyina	gyi.na
Gyurme	'gyur.med

H

Hemi	hemis

J

Jadral	bya.bral
Jamgon	'jam.mgon
Jampa	byams.pa
Jampal	'jam.dpal
Jamyang	'jam.dbyang
Jatson	'ja'.tshon
Jaypa	'byed.pa
Jetsun	rje.btsun
Jigdrel	'jigs.bral
Jigme	'jigs.med
Jigten	'jigs.rten
Jomo	jo.mo
Jonangpa	jo.nang.pa
Ju	ju
Jungnay	'byung.nas
Jyang	byang

K

Kachod	mkha'.spyod
Kochodpa	mkha'.spyod.pa
Kadampa	bka'.gdams.pa
Kadzod	bka'.mdzod
Kagyu	bka'.brgyud
Kagyupa	bka'.brgyud.pa
Kalzang	skal.bzang
Kampo	kam.po
Kaṃtshang	kaṃ.tshang
Kangkar	kang.dkar
Kanjur	bka'.'gyur
Karma	karma
Karmapa	karma.pa
Katok	ka.thog
Kawa	ka.ba
Kaycha	kas.cha
Khakhyab	mkha'.khyab
Kham	khams
Khampa	khams.pa
Khamtrul	khams.sprul
Khanchen	mkhan.chen
Khandro	mkha'.'gro
Khenpo	mkhan.po
Khon	mkhon
Khyab	skyabs
Khyenpa	mkhyen.pa
Khyentse	mkhyen.brtse
Khyungpo	khyung.po
Konchog	dkon.mchog
Kongjo	kong.jo
Kongpo	kong.po
Kongtrul	kong.sprul
Kunchen	kun.mkhyen
Kunden	kun.ldan
Kundrol	kun.sgrol
Kunga	kun.dga'
Kungba	kung.ba
Kunkhyen	kun.mkhyen
Kunrig	kun.rig
Kuntu	kun.tu
Kunzang	kun.bzang
Kunzig	kun.bzig
Kyi	skyid

L

Lab	brlabs
Lama	bla.ma
Lawang	bla.dbang
Legdrup	legs.'grub
Lekshay	legs.bshad
Lesom	le.som
Lha	lha
Lhachen	lha.chen

Lhakhang	lha.khang
Lhamo	lha.mo
Lharje	lha.rje
Lhasa	lha.sa
Lhatheg	lha.theg
Lhodrak	lho.brag
Lhundrup	lhun.grub
Lhunpo	lhun.po
Ling	gling
Lingje	gling.rje
Lingpa	gling.pa
Lobzang	blo.bzang
Lodro	blo.gros
Long	klong
Longchen	klong.chen
Longchenpa	klong.chen.pa
Lopon	slob.dpon
Lotsawa	lo.tsā.ba

M

Machig	ma.gcig
Machu	ma.chu
Mal	mal
Mar	mar
Marpa	mar.pa
Mase	rma.se
Meton	me.ston
Mikyo	mi.bskyod
Milarepa	mi.la.ras.pa
Mindrol	smin.grol
Minjur	mi.'gyur
Minling	smin.gling
Minyak	mi.nyag
Mipham	mi.pham
Monlagar-chung	mon.la.gar.chung
Mowa	mo.ba

N

Nakchu	nag.chu
Naljor	rnal.'byor
Namgyal	rnam.rgyal
Namtsho	nam.gtsho
Namtshowa	gnam.mtsho.ba
Nangchen	nang.chen
Nangdon	snang.don
Nangwa	snang.ba
Nedo	gnas.mdo
Nenang	gnas.nang
Ngagdzod	sngags.mdzod
Ngakphu	ngags.phu
Ngal	bsngal
Ngawang	ngag.dbang
Ngok	rngog
Ngom	ngom
Ngompa	ngom.pa
Ngonpa	ngon.pa
Ngorpa	ngor.pa
Norbu	nor.bu
Nuden	nu.ldan
Nyendrup	snyen.sgrub
Nyenpa	snyen.pa
Nyenre	snyan.ras
Nyima	nyi.ma
Nyinche	nyin.byed
Nyinchen	nyin.chen
Nying	rnying
Nyingche	snying.che
Nyingma	rnying.ma
Nyingpo	snying.po
Nyugrumpa	snyug.rum.pa

O

Ogmin	'og.min
Ozer	'od.zer

P

Pakshi	pak.shi
Pal	dpal
Palchen	dpal.chen
Paldrup	dpal.grub
Paljor	dpal.'byor
Palpung	dpal.spungs
Paltseg	dpal.gtseg
Pangphug	spang.phug
Parma	'par.ma
Patsap	dpal.tshab
Pawo	dpa'.bo
Phadampa	pha.dam.pa
Phagmo	phag.mo
Phakpa	'phags.pa
Phen-yul	'phan.yul
Pholha	pho.lha
Phowa	'pho.ba
Phuntsog	phun.tshogs
Pomdrakpa	spon.brag.pa
Ponlob	dpon.slob
Pungri	spungs.ri

R

Rabjampa	rab.'byams.pa
Rabten	rab.sten
Radeng	rwa.deng
Rangjung	rang.byung
Rawa	rwa.ba
Rechen	ras.chen
Rechungpa	ras.chung.pa
Rekarwa	ras.dkar.ba
Rewa	re.ba
Rigden	rigs.ldan
Rigdzin	rig.'dzin
Rigpa	rig.pa
Rigpe	rig.pa'i
Rinchen	rin.chen
Rinpoche	rin.po.che
Rinpung	rin.spungs
Riwa	ri.ba
Riwoche	ri.bo.che
Rolpe	rol.pa'i
Rongtonpa	rong.ston.pa
Rumtek	rum.gtegs

S

Sachen	sa.chen
Sakya	sa.skya
Sakyapa	sa.skya.pa
Salmo	gsal.mo
Samding	bsam.ldings
Samdrup	bsam.'grub
Samten	bsam.gtan
Samye	bsam.yas
Sandu	sa.'du
Sang Ngag	gsang.sngags
Sangphu	gsang.phu
Sangye	sangs.rgyas
Senge	seng.ge
Ser	gser
Sera	gse.ra
Shamar	zhwa.dmar
Shamarpa	zhwa.dmar.pa
Shangpa	shangs.pa
Sharchog	shar.phyogs
Shau	sha.'ug
Shedrup	bshad.sgrub
Shegpa	gshegs.pa
Sheja	shes.bya
Shelkar	shel.dkar
Sherab	shes.rab
Shi	shi
Shijay	shi.'byed
Shu	shod
Situ	si.tu
Situpa	si.tu.pa

Solo	so.lo
Sonam	bsod.nams
Sangphu	gsang.phu
Sowa	gso.ba
Srongtsen	srongs.btsan
Suchu	su.chu
Surmang	zur.mang

T

Taglung	stag.lung
Tago	stag.sgo
Taksham	stag.sham
Talep	khra.leb
Tanjur	bstan.'gyur
Tarangpa	ta.rang.pa
Tashi	bkra.shis
Tawa	lta.ba
Teng	steng
Tengwa	phreng.ba
Tenkyong	bstan.skyong
Tenpa	bstan.pa
Tendzin	bstan.'dzin
Terdzod	gter.mdzod
Terma	gter.ma
Terton	gter.ston
Tewo	tre.bo
Thanglha	thang.lha
Thangpa	thang.pa
Thangtong	thang.stong
Thargye	thar.rgyas
Thaye	mtha'.yas
Thegchog	theg.mchog
Thinley	'phrin.las
Thobjay	thob.rgyas
Thodrol	thos.'grol
Thokar	thod.dkar
Thongwa	mthong.ba
Thubten	thub.bstan
Tingri	ting.ri
Togden	rtogs.ldan
Topga	stobs.dga'
Tray	dre
Trichen	khri.chen
Tridzin	khri.'dzin
Trisong	khri.bsrong
Trung	drung
Tsalpa	tshal.pa
Tsang	gtsang
Tsangpa	gtsang.pa
Tsari	tsa.ri
Tsarpa	tshar.pa
Tse	tse
Tsechu	tshes.bcu
Tsemo	rtse.mo
Tseringma	tse.ring.ma
Tsewang	tshe.dbang
Tsogyal	mtsho.rgyal
Tsondru	tson.'grus
Tsongkhapa	gtsong.kha.pa
Tsonpo	tshon.po
Tsuglak	gtsug.lag
Tsultim	tshul.khrims
Tsurphu	mtshur.phu
Tulku	sprul.sku
Tup	thub

U

U	dbu
Urgyen	o.rgyan
Urgyenpa	o.rgyan.pa

W

Wangchuk	dbang.phyug
Wangkyi	dbang.kyi
Wangmo	dbang.mo
Wangpo	dbang.po

Y

Yagde	yag.sde
Yangbachen	yang.ba.can
Yanglayshod	yang.le.shod
Yarlung	g.yar.lung
Yenlag	yan.lag
Yeshe	ye.shes
Yongdzin	yong.'dzin
Yongtonpa	g.yung.ston.pa
Yudrakpa	g.yu.brag.pa

Z

Zabmo	zab.mo
Zangpo	bzang.po
Zechen	ze.chen
Zhang	zhang
Zhingta	zhing.rta
Zhonnu	gzhon.nu

BIBLIOGRAPHY

TIBETAN SOURCES

kam.tshang.sdom.rgyun.rnaṃ.thar.mdor.bsdus.tshul.khrims.mdses.rgyan by Karma Trakpa Yongdu

karma.kam.tshang.brgyud.pa.rin.po.che.nam.par.thar.pa.rab.'byams.nor.bu.zla.ba.chu.shel.gyi.phreng.ba. (Two volumes: 1699 C.E. and 1774 C.E.) by Situ Mahāpaṇḍita Tenpi Nyinchi and Bay Lotsawa, Tsewang Kunkhyab

mkhas.pa'i.dga.ston by the second Pawo Rinpoche, Tsuklak Tengwa

rgyal.ba.zhwa.dmar.nag.gi.rnam.thar.mdor.bsdus by Drupon Tenzin Rinpoche

chos.rje.karma.pa.sku.'phreng.rim.byon.gyi.rnam.thar.mdor.bsdus.dpag.bsam.'khri.shing by Mendong Tshampa Rinpoche, Ngaydon Tenjay

chos.byong.bstan.pa'i.padma.jay.pa'i.nying.che by Padma Karpo

deb.ther.sngon.po by 'Gos Lotsawa, Zhonu Pal

rnying.ma'i.chos.'byung by Dudjom Rinpoche

mtsungs.mi.bla.ma.chos.rje.karma.pa.rim.byon.kyi.tun.mon.gi.rnam.par.thar.pa by Karma Ngelek

ENGLISH SOURCES

Douglas, N., and White, M. *Karmapa: The Black Hat Lama of Tibet.* London: Luzac, 1976.

Richardson, Hugh. "The Karmapa Sect: An Historical Note." *Journal of the Royal Asiatic Society,* 1958.

Snellgrove, David, and Richardson, Hugh. *A Cultural History of Tibet.* Boulder: Prajñā Press, 1980.

9 781570 626449

Printed in the United States
by Baker & Taylor Publisher Services